LEGAL LYNCHING

LEGAL LYNCHING

The Death Penalty

and America's Future

Rev. Jesse L. Jackson, Sr.

Representative Jesse L. Jackson, Jr.

Bruce Shapiro

THE NEW PRESS

NEW YORK

Published in the United States by The New Press, New York, 2001
Distributed by W. W. Norton & Company, Inc., New York

LIBRARY OF CONGRESS CATALOGING-IN-PUBLICATION DATA
Jackson, Jesse.
Legal lynching : the death penalty and America's future / Rev. Jesse L. Jackson, Sr.,
Representative Jesse L. Jackson, Jr., Bruce Shapiro.
p.   cm.
Includes bibliographical references and index.
ISBN 1-56584-685-0 (hc.)
1. Capital punishment—United States.   I. Jackson, Jesse.
II. Shapiro, Bruce.   III. Title.
HV8699.U5 J35 2001
364.66'0973—dc21   2001034256

The New Press was established in 1990 as a not-for-profit alternative to the large,
commercial publishing houses currently dominating the book publishing industry.
The New Press operates in the public interest rather than for private gain,
and is committed to publishing, in innovative ways, works of educational, cultural,
and community value that are often deemed insufficiently profitable.

The New Press, 450 West 41st Street, 6th floor, New York, NY 10036
www.thenewpress.com

Design by Kathryn Parise

Printed in the United States of America

2   4   6   8   10   9   7   5   3   1

CONTENTS

Contents

ACKNOWLEDGMENTS

This book stands on the shoulders of death-row litigators and criminal-justice scholars. In particular, anyone attempting to write about capital punishment is in irredeemable debt to decades of tireless scholarship by Hugo Adam Bedau of Tufts University, and to his essential sourcebook, *The Death Penalty in America* (Oxford University Press). James Megivern's *The Death Penalty: An Historical and Theological Survey* (Paulist Press) greatly illuminates the debate over capital punishment within Western religious traditions. The Death Penalty Information Center; the Sentencing Project; the Center on Crime, Communities and Culture of the Open Society Institute; and the Quixote Center of Hyattsville, Maryland, all provided crucial data and reports.

Margaret Spillane contributed the "Sleeping Lawyer Syndrome" diagnosis, and much else, to this book. Particular thanks to George Seymour and the staff of the Illinois Second Congressional District office; John Mitchell and other staff of Rainbow/PUSH; to Victor Navasky, Katrina vanden Heuvel, and the editors of the *Nation*; David Talbot, Joan Walsh, and the editors of Salon.com; Aoife Spillane-Hinks; Rob Warden, executive director of the Center on Wrongful Convictions, Northwestern University.

Joel Joseph of National Press Books first conceived of this book's predecessor volume, *Legal Lynching: Racism, Injustice and the*

Death Penalty. Mr. Joseph was instrumental in the creation, writing and publication of that earlier and different work, for which the authors of the present book are grateful. Frank Watkins was also essential to this predecessor volume.

The present book would not exist without Andy Hsiao and André Schiffrin of The New Press, who conceived the project and brought it to fruition on a remarkably tight schedule.

The authors also thank: Stephen Bright of the Southern Center for Human Rights; George Kendall of the NAACP Legal Defense and Education Fund; Michael Mello of Vermont School of Law; Pamela S. Karlan of Stanford University Law School; Robert Burt, Drew Days III, and Harlon Dalton of Yale University Law School; Franz Allina of the New York State Capital Defenders Project; pioneering moratorium campaigner and vindicated death-row inmate Delbert Tibbs; Governor George Ryan of Illinois; Frank Ochberg, M.D., of the Dart Foundation; the Most Rev. Peter Rosazza, Auxiliary Bishop of the Archdiocese of Hartford; Andrew Martin of the New York Bar Association; and the staff of Sterling Memorial Library, Yale University, and the Lillian Goldman Library, Yale School of Law.

PREFACE

Before the state of Texas killed Gary Graham on June 23, 2000, Graham asked me to visit with him. So for an hour, we talked and prayed. I had first become aware of Graham's case in 1993. That year, Václav Havel, Bishop Desmond Tutu, and others around the globe asked Texas to spare his life. Now it was seven years later, and he had only hours to live. Though the prison functionaries in Huntsville were already preparing the death chamber, there were no tears. Somehow, Gary Graham, after 17 years on death row, had found an inner sense of peace. He felt, he told me, that he was being used as a change agent—to expose the American death-penalty system to the world.

Gary Graham's execution is one of those stories that raises nothing but the most troubling questions. In 1981, he was just 17 years old—a kid who'd endured severe abuse by his father—when he was arrested for shooting Bobby Lambert during a nighttime stickup in a Houston parking lot. The teenaged Graham denied being in the parking lot that night. No physical evidence linked him to Lambert's murder. Six eyewitnesses saw the murder—but only one, sitting in her car across the parking lot, identified Graham. The others, including three closer to the shooting, either could not identify him or said Graham was definitely not Lambert's killer.

How, with such weak and ambiguous evidence, did a teenager

end up on Texas' death row? The usual ways. The police wanted a suspect, any suspect, and Graham—who had admitted to several robberies—fit the bill. The fact that witnesses described an African-American like Graham didn't hurt. His low-rent trial lawyer—one of the worst in the state—didn't bother to present a defense. The so-called defense investigator later admitted that both he and Graham's lawyer "assumed Gary was guilty from the start" and they "just went through the motions." When a new lawyer finally tracked down those witnesses years later, three of the jurors who sentenced him to die filed affidavits saying they would never have voted to convict if that evidence had been available.

The Book of Deuteronomy says it's a sin to kill on the basis of one witness. Yet in Texas, Gary Graham was about to die on the basis of one witness, a witness who said she saw him 19 years earlier through a windshield. In that Bible-toting country, Deuteronomy's injunction meant nothing in the face of the desire for vengeance.

When Graham and I talked, his case had already gone through a final appeal to the Texas Board of Pardons and Paroles. The members of this board get paid an annual salary by the taxpayers, yet never meet. They communicate by fax and email. They never see who is going to die. They are partisan political appointees, in a state where politicians have believed it popular to risk killing innocent individuals. Then there was the U.S. Supreme Court. Four justices voted to delay the execution so federal courts could investigate Graham's possible innocence, but five justices turned their backs. One vote between life and death.

Gary Graham asked me to witness his execution. He struggled as guards strapped him to the gurney. In the death chamber, he gave his final statement—still insisting upon his innocence. With the poison already in his veins he spoke to me in his last breath:

"They are killing me tonight. They are murdering me tonight." And then silence. Walking out of that prison, past the gate and the guards and the protesters, I wept bitterly that the state could use its extraordinary power to make a point at the expense of one man.

A half-year later, I was in Oklahoma meeting Governor Frank Keating and his officials about the case of Wanda Jean Allen. Different issues, same outcome. Wanda Jean Allen was a woman with an IQ of 67. She shot her lover, who herself had a record as a killer, after an argument in front of a police station. It was clearly a crime of passion; there was no premeditation. When Wanda Jean appealed her death sentence, to the state parole board, the prosecutor wrote that she'd been to college. It turned out that although Wanda Jean had once said she went to college, in fact she dropped out in the ninth grade—and the prosecutors knew that. Everyone in the room knew she was retarded. Yet in the end they voted for vengeance; in my view that day, it was nothing short of state-sanctioned murder.

The circumstances of Wanda Jean Allen's death sentence, like Gary Graham's, trouble a good many people. Execution of the mentally retarded, execution in the face of evidence of innocence—both challenge our faith in the justice system. We are also finally waking up to just how profoundly capital punishment is shaped by race. In 1994 I pleaded along with many others for South Carolina officials to save the life of Susan Smith, who had falsely claimed a black man had killed her children. They listened, and she is alive today. But a month later, also in South Carolina, there was another case: a young black man who was mentally retarded, who had killed another young man. The victim's mother pleaded for his killer's life, but South Carolina ignored her. The same people who accepted my letter on behalf of a white woman killed this young black man.

As the parole board and governor deliberated over the life of Wanda Jean Allen, I found my mind turning to another case of a woman facing capital punishment under color of law. This case is in the Bible, and it shows perfectly why the death penalty is such a politically charged issue. Early one morning Jesus went walking at the Mount of Olives and then returned to the temple, to the crowd of people waiting for him to teach. When he got there, according to the Gospel of John, "the scribes and the Pharisees brought a woman who had been caught in the act of adultery," placing her in the midst of the crowd. The scribes and the Pharisees said to Jesus, "Teacher, this woman has been caught in the act of adultery. Now in the law Moses commanded us to stone such. What do you say about her?" They did this, John tells us, "to test him, that they might have some charge to bring against him."

What were the Pharisees and scribes—the religious leaders and the media of their day—demanding of Jesus? They were demanding that he pass the same capital-punishment test that is imposed upon today's politicians. This woman, they were saying, violated the civil law, she violated the religious law, and the law says she must die. Will you stand by her death sentence? they asked him over and over, and the crowd gathered its stones.

How did Jesus reply? According to John, "He stood up and said to them: 'Let him who is without sin among you be the first to throw a stone at her.' " The Bible says that when he did that, they put their stones down—"one by one, beginning with the eldest."

What Jesus did that day was stand by a person condemned to capital punishment. It was not the easy thing, the politic thing, to do. The religious order, the political order, the media—all demanded her death. To stand with a person accused of murder, a person on death row—even a person like Wanda Jean Allen, who has clearly violated the law—is always a version of the same test faced by Jesus that day.

The Bible also describes a politician for whom the death penalty was a test of leadership: Pontius Pilate, the governor of Judea. Jesus had been born under a death warrant; his life ended with a makeshift trial and death row. It was up to Pilate to decide whether to spare Jesus, whom he knew to be innocent. Though it was Pilate "in the judgment seat," Pilate who had the authority, he would not make up his mind. So he asked his wife and he asked the crowd: in other words, he would not make a move until he consulted the polls. And the crowd had been deliberately whipped up by the elders, says the Gospel, because Jesus' execution was to their political advantage. What we learn from this story—as from Gary Graham's and Wanda Jean Allen's—is that when nations are consumed with blood thoughts, when leaders deliberately play the death-penalty card, the innocent and the guilty alike are caught by the same mob psychology.

Standing with those on death row is never easy. I have my own moments of uncertainty, when the violence of which individuals are capable seems overwhelming. But the issue for me—as for a growing number of others—is the cost of state-sanctioned killing. Consider even the coldest and most calculating crime in our recent history, the Oklahoma City bombing. Even before the FBI identified Timothy McVeigh, the government announced it would seek the death penalty for the perpetrator of the bombing. For the next several years, the promise was that McVeigh's execution would bring "closure." Yet after his sentencing, it became clear that McVeigh actively sought his own execution, trying to make himself into a perverse martyr. The media had a field day. Then as his execution date approached, it was revealed that even in the largest and most publicized domestic terrorism trial of all time, law enforcement had managed to withhold evidence. Far from ensuring closure, McVeigh's death sentence sucked the system down a hole.

Thinking about capital punishment in the face of a horrendous crime like that in Oklahoma City, I also remember the German Protestant theologian Martin Niemöller, who spoke of the cost of failing to speak up for the least popular—in the case of Nazi Germany, for Communists and Catholics and Jews. "When they came for me," he said, "there was no one left to speak up." Death row is the embodiment of Niemöller's dictum; no one is more unpopular than a person convicted, justly or not, of horrendous crime, and ending the death penalty can seem a hopeless cause.

Yet the message even from Oklahoma City is that the views of Americans can undergo profound change when they are presented with the facts about the system. This is evident from many other issues. For instance, for years, only a few Americans spoke out against apartheid in South Africa and called for freeing Nelson Mandela from prison. Our government considered him a terrorist, and Congress would not support his release. But the more the American public saw of apartheid, the more people learned about that system and about Mandela, the more his support grew. It took a quarter century, but today Nelson Mandela is universally revered and apartheid universally reviled as a moral abomination. There is no reason to think that the American death penalty is immune to that long arc of education, activism, and reform. As the public learns more about the abuses and failures of the death-penalty system, opponents of capital punishment become less isolated.

Capital punishment offers a fundamental moral challenge. When you stand with people on death row, you are—like Jesus—

facing down the political order, the press, and the polls. Somehow, a growing number of Americans, who see all of our rights jeopardized by the national rush to vengeance and execution, are finding the capacity to do just that—to stand with those on death row.

Rev. Jesse L. Jackson, Sr.

LEGAL
LYNCHING

INTRODUCTION

America Faces Its

Nightmare

Here is an American nightmare. You are at home one night when the police break down your door, place you in handcuffs, and accuse you of murdering an elderly couple—a crime of which you have never heard. Now add this to the nightmare: You are mentally retarded and cannot read or write. The local sheriff has arrested you to distract attention from his own corruption. Your defense lawyer has never tried a murder case and deals drugs in his spare time. Your trial is all over in three days. A career con artist testifies that you confessed in jail, a confession you never uttered. The prosecutor knows there is no evidence and knows you are mentally impaired, but hides that knowledge from the judge and jury.

As you are sentenced to die, you insist upon your innocence, but even your own lawyer does not believe you. From the shadow land of death row—confined to your cell 24 hours a day except for three hours per week of exercise—you protest. It doesn't matter. In two weeks' time, the prison's medical staff and guards and

1

chaplain and officials will feed you a sedative and strap you to a gurney, utter a prayer over your head, and insert intravenous needles in your arms to receive a poison that will halt your breath and your heart.

This was Ronnie Burrell's American nightmare, in every detail. He awakened from it only on January 2, 2001, when he walked away from the death row of Angola State Penitentiary in Louisiana with $10 prison-issue bus fare in his pocket, 14 years after being arrested with a friend for a murder neither of them committed, four years after coming within a fortnight of execution.

Ronnie Burrell shares his nightmare with nearly 100 others exonerated and freed from death row in recent years. One of them is a man named Anthony Porter. On the surface, the two men have little in common: Burrell, a white man from rural Louisiana; Porter, an African-American from Chicago. But they were both born poor. Both reached adulthood with judgment and ambitions defined by mental impairment: Like Ronnie Burrell, Anthony Porter's IQ is barely above 50. Neither Ronnie Burrell nor Anthony Porter might seem the stuff of which revolutions are made. Yet these individuals and others like them are responsible for a seismic shift in the politics of the death penalty, the subject of this book.

Anthony Porter's story tells you much of what you need to know about the death penalty in America. In 1982, Chicago police arrested 26-year-old Porter for a double homicide in Washington Park. No physical evidence linked him to the crime, but an eyewitness picked his photo from a lineup book and the police—without further investigation—decided they had their man. The court shipped Porter, still maintaining his innocence, off to Illinois' death row.

In 1996, Porter came within two days of the needle when a

federal judge issued a temporary stay to consider Porter's mental impairment. It was not until then—after 12 years on death row—that Anthony Porter found a few people who took seriously his cry of innocence. But it wasn't judges, or police officers, or ministers. It was a handful of journalism students at Northwestern University, students whose class project was to treat Porter as if he really were innocent until proven guilty. Those college students started doing the work that the cops and prosecutors and defense lawyers hadn't bothered with: interviewing witnesses, reconstructing the crime scene. They found the real murderer, and got his confession on tape.

Anthony Porter's exoneration—and his hairbreadth escape from execution—shocked Illinois and the nation, all the more so because he was the thirteenth innocent man to escape Illinois' death row since 1977. Because of Anthony Porter, the *Chicago Tribune* began poring over every death-penalty case in Illinois and found a grim parade of error and racial discrimination, including 33 death sentences handed down to defendants whose lawyers were subsequently suspended or disbarred. Because of Anthony Porter, in January of 2000 Illinois' Republican governor George Ryan—citing what he called "a shameful record of convicting innocent people and putting them on death row"—imposed a moratorium on that state's executions, the first of its kind anywhere.

Porter's case and Illinois' moratorium were two tremors foretelling a national earthquake. A Gallup Poll in February of 2000 revealed that support for capital punishment had plummeted to its lowest level in two decades. Recent statewide surveys in Kentucky and Texas, and a national ABC News survey, show even more dramatic shifts.

As we write it is a year since Illinois imposed its moratorium, and in that time the number of fully exonerated death-row inmates nationwide has risen to at least 86. Eighty-six of the walking dead, freed in Texas, Illinois, Florida, Virginia, Oklahoma. Every day, their stories collide in the headlines with news of more executions: a contradiction jarring even to Americans who have until now always supported the death penalty. Even as violent crime and homicide stand at their lowest ebb since the the 1950s, politicians prescribe death for more and more crimes. Even as more individuals are sentenced to die than at any time since the Great Depression, exposés of massive death-row injustice proliferate: intoxicated and sleeping defense lawyers, lying prosecutors, all-white juries. Even as science provides new techniques for proving innocence and guilt, the Supreme Court and Congress strip condemned prisoners of their rights to appeal and to get new evidence heard.

All these contradictions leave many Americans feeling a kind of moral dissonance. Because of that, debate over capital punishment is rapidly approaching a tipping point that transcends the conventional Republican-Democrat, liberal-conservative divide. As this book is being written, the U.S. Congress is considering several different measures to slow down the machinery of death, including a national moratorium on executions (a measure sponsored by one of the authors). More than 30 municipalities—including cities and towns in the traditionally pro–capital punishment South—had passed resolutions urging such a moratorium nationwide, a moratorium embraced by some conservatives and longtime supporters of the death penalty such as columnist George Will.

Why is the tide turning? Americans' past support for the death penalty cannot come from cruelty, surely, for most Americans are not cruel people. Instead it begins with a longing for security and justice. People have believed the death penalty is a deterrent; they have believed it vindicates victims; they have believed that only the truly deserving die, that the courts protect the innocent. They have believed that capital punishment is an integral part of American and Judeo-Christian tradition.

But the sheer volume and pace of state-sponsored killing has profoundly undercut each of these premises. The year 2000 brought 85 executions, more than four times the number of executions in 1990. In 1992 it was news when presidential candidate Bill Clinton interrupted his campaign to approve the execution of brain-damaged Rickie Ray Rector in Arkansas; in the 2000 presidential campaign, executions were so routine for George W. Bush—he approved 126 of them during his tenure as Texas' governor—that it became news only when he briefly delayed the execution of one inmate for DNA testing. So frequent were the executions in Texas that if Bush had taken a solemn sabbatical for each killing he would never have been able to campaign.

As the executions escalate and as death sentences proliferate, the public is confronted with the facts: the facts of racial bias, shoddy lawyering, corrupt law enforcement, bad forensic science, and most of all by the sheer absence of mercy and forgiveness. As a result, uneasy Americans, in all parts of the country and on all sides of the political spectrum, now question their own assumptions about capital punishment. A growing number are changing their minds, much like the late Supreme Court Justice Harry Blackmun. In 1976 Justice Blackmun voted with the Supreme Court majority that reinstated capital punishment four years after executions were halted by an earlier decision. In the next several years Blackmun continued to vote to uphold death sentences in some key cases. But by the time of his retirement in 1994, Justice Blackmun had become convinced that the vast inequities of American society make a just and fair death penalty impossible. "I will

5

no longer cooperate with the machinery of death," Justice Blackmun wrote.

The change is evident everywhere. Investigative reporters have made death row a regular beat, exposing massive abuses of the justice system on the way to the execution chamber. A growing chorus of murder victims' families who oppose execution is another extraordinary factor: people like Bud Welch, whose daughter Jennifer was killed by Timothy McVeigh's bomb in Oklahoma City, or like the parents of Matthew Shepard, the gay college student hung from a fence and beaten to death in Laramie, Wyoming, who asked that Wyoming prosecutors not seek the death penalty for their son's killers. Such voices challenge the idea that execution brings "closure" to families. Another pivotal moment came with Texas' killing of Karla Faye Tucker, a devout born-again Christian whose cause was taken up by evangelist Pat Robertson. As the first woman to face execution in decades, Karla Faye Tucker was accorded a rare privilege for death-row inmates: telling her story to a national prime-time television audience, entering America's living rooms as a flawed and troubled human being. America's unusual encounter with the essential humanity of a single death-row inmate did not save Karla Faye Tucker's life, but it led Robertson and some other religious conservatives to question capital punishment and endorse a moratorium on further executions.

After decades as lonely voices of witness and dissent, death-penalty opponents now have an opportunity to build a true majority, to end the American capital-punishment nightmare. But that means taking seriously many Americans' concerns for a safe society, for the rights of victims and their families. It demands a national conversation about how those legitimate concerns can be severed from the unreviewable vengeance and brutality of state-sponsored murder. And it requires fresh arguments to illustrate anew something most of us opposed to the death penalty simply take for granted: the profound failure of American ideals reflected in the system of government-sponsored killing, the racism and economic injustice embedded in a prison-industrial complex of which capital punishment is the most violent expression.

This book is a tool for all Americans engaged in the new debate over the death penalty. It explores the myths and realities of capital punishment in American history, challenges old assumptions with new facts, and tries to light a way out of the American nightmare—beginning, but not ending, with a moratorium on state-sponsored killing. This book is for people who have supported the death penalty in years past but now find themselves troubled by the record number of executions and the revelations of death-row frame-ups. It is for people who have always thought that the death penalty is murder, but who now seek for the first time to get involved, to raise this vital issue in their own houses of worship, schools, and communities. It is for dedicated capital-punishment abolitionists and activists—communities of faith, students, attorneys, prisoners and their families—already working to save lives in a rapidly shifting political climate.

Most death-row inmates will never share Anthony Porter's and Ronnie Burrell's good fortune at awakening from the American nightmare. Most will instead share the fate of Odell Barnes of Texas, convicted of the 1989 rape and murder of Helen Bass of Wichita County when he was 19 years old. Although his defense lawyer never investigated, Barnes maintained his innocence, and years after his conviction, appellate lawyers conducting the first serious inquiry into his case found contradictory witnesses, indications that police had planted evidence, and numerous other irregularities. A succession of courts found that Barnes could not introduce such critical evidence under the rigid law of Texas, which requires that new evidence be presented within just 30 days of conviction. Unlike the death-row inmates of Illinois, Odell Barnes found no forbearance from Texas' then-Governor Bush, despite direct pleas from Pope John Paul II, French president Lionel Jospin, and others. Texas killed Barnes by lethal injection on March 1, 2000.

America stands at a crossroads. It is a crossroads between finality and fairness, between irredeemable error and justice, between life and death. More and more Americans, finding themselves at this crossroads, are looking at cases like Anthony Porter's and Ronnie Burrell's and Wanda Jean Allen's and declaring that enough is enough. The question is not just the fate of falsely condemned inmates like Burrell and Porter, or of those whose responsibility is mitigated by mental defect like Wanda Jean Allen. In the long run, the question is how the criminal-justice system treats even the most brutally guilty. Evidence suggests that a majority of Americans are ready to look at that question with new compassion. In the meantime, it is time for urgent national reconsideration of a death-penalty machine that fails to deliver on the most basic premises of fairness and justice.

CHAPTER 1

The Death Penalty and

the American Past

It is August 6, 1890. Ninteenth-century America is waking up to the power of twentieth-century technology, to the first lightbulbs, phonographs, telephones, automobiles.

In the basement of Auburn State Penitentiary in upstate New York, a man named William Kemmler is bound to a chair with heavy leather straps. His journey there has attracted international attention, and this day more than 100 reporters are on hand. An illiterate who confessed to the ax-murder killing of his lover in an alcohol-sodden rage, Kemmler is the guinea pig in an unprece-dented experiment: the first attempt to execute a criminal with electricity. The medieval gallows would give way to a punishment both more modern and, its proponents argued, more humane.

Among the people most anxiously awaiting the results of today's experiment are the industrialist Thomas Edison and his great rival George Westinghouse. Edison and Westinghouse have developed different electric-power systems, and Edison has been promoting his as safer for consumers. Since the Auburn electric chair's generator is manufactured by Westinghouse, Edison views Kemmler's execution as a PR bonanza, and even suggests that capital punishment be renamed "Westinghousing." George Westinghouse, for his part, is so worried about the bad press that he has poured $100,000 into Kemmler's unsuccessful legal appeals, all the way up to the U.S. Supreme Court.

At a sign from Auburn's warden, a guard pulls a switch. Sixteen hundred volts of current run through Kemmler's body. His body still, the witnesses in Auburn's basement conclude Kemmler is dead—until a doctor feels a faint pulse. The condemned man begins to groan and foam at the mouth, driving sickened witnesses from the room. Quickly, the warden orders the switch pulled again; the next jolt burns Kemmler's scalp and this time, the doctor finds, he is definitively dead.

Edison, awaiting word at his home, tells reporters, "I should have been excited myself" to be at Auburn. But an electrician listed as one of the official witnesses that day has a different view. Charles Huntley, manager of the Brush Electric Light Company in Buffalo, tells reporters that the new "electric chair" is nothing short of legal torture. "It was one of the most horrifying sights I have ever witnessed or expect to witness," he says. "There is no money that would tempt me to go through the business again."

Capital punishment, at times, seems as much an unchanging fixture of the American landscape as the sheer bluffs of Monument Valley in Utah, where so many Westerns were filmed—complete with the familiar hanging scenes. Politicians make it seem as if the death penalty is part of our national heritage, as if opposition to capital punishment is nothing but an invention of 1960s liberals.

"The Constitution . . . authorizes the death penalty," writes pro-execution legal scholar Ernst Van Den Haag, adding that the framers of the Constitution "did not think that taking the life of a murderer is inconsistent with 'the sanctity of life.' " Such "original intent" arguments have succeeded in many people's minds in wrapping the death penalty in the American flag.

But as the story of William Kemmler suggests, the reality is more complicated. Kemmler's story reminds us that the death penalty has evolved for reasons that often have little to do with law and order. Edison's gloating and electrician Huntley's revulsion at the dawn of the modern execution era mark the two poles of debate over capital punishment. This debate has deeply marked American history; pushing and pulling over capital punishment have played a crucial role in shaping the law as we know it today, and opposition to capital punishment is as much a part of American tradition as the Fourth of July. So it is time to retell the story: Any discussion of the death penalty in today's America must begin with an accurate framing of the death penalty in the American past.

Capital punishment arrived on North American shores with the very first British colonists. It was scant weeks after the establishment of Jamestown in 1608 that colonists carried out their first hanging: an accused mutineer named George Kendall. British law in that period routinely handed out death sentences even for minor crimes like robbery and burglary. On paper, the colonies followed suit: "If any person commit Burglary, or rob any person, he shall be branded on the right hand with the Letter B—for 2nd offence, shall be branded on his left hand, and whipt, and for the third offence he shall be put to death," read the 1656 Laws of the New Haven Colony. In Puritan New England, the colonists added some capital offenses of their own to their so-called Blue Laws, prescribing the death penalty for adultery, homosexuality, and for persistently "stubborn" children.

By the time British colonists settled in North America, capital punishment had for centuries been an escalating public spectacle in Europe. Early Christian theologians debated the legitimacy of the death penalty, and some feudal rulers such as William the Conqueror opposed its use. But by medieval times, executions—both by church and crown—became more indiscriminate, and torture often accompanied death. The number of capital crimes increased, too; in England, for example, a death writ condemning heretics to burn or drown stayed on the books from 1382 to 1677. French nobles at least had the comfort of knowing they would be honorably beheaded with an ax rather than being hanged or drawn and quartered—often how members of the lower classes would meet their demise. Women were usually strangled to death and burned to ashes out of a sense of "decency" to their gender. (It would have been improper to make a public spectacle of a woman's bare limbs, whether attached to her body or otherwise.) Henry VIII made boiling to death a legal form of execution, and more than 72,000 of his subjects were killed by this and other means. By the seventeenth century, no less than 200,000 women had been executed as witches throughout Europe. Bodies were left on display for weeks and sometimes months.

Despite this bloody history and the severity of the American colonies' laws, in practice, as legal historian Lawrence Silberman puts it, "the colonies used the death penalty pretty sparingly." True, there were notorious executions like those following the Salem witchcraft trials in the 1690s. But for much of colonial America, many capital laws were honored only in the breach. In some cases, the colonists outright refused to invoke capital punishment. By the 1650s, juries were declining to convict adulterers because citizens found the death penalty disproportionate: the first instances on record of so-called jury nullification, the same citizen-refusal to convict under unjust laws that in the 1730s helped establish the uniquely American institution of free speech, and that today has led to occasional juries refusing convictions under disproportionate drug laws. Capital punishment for sodomy was next, its enforcement ending after 1673.

In fact, despite our image of angry Puritans hanging witches by the wagonload, the first 40 years of the Massachusetts Bay Colony brought only 15 executions for all offenses, an average of one every two and a half years. In Pennsylvania, executions averaged just one per year all the way up through the Revolution. What is more, colonial governors showed a far greater degree of compassion than most death-penalty states' governors today. In the eighteenth century, more than half of New York's condemned were spared, and the governors of Virginia pardoned or commuted the sentence of one-quarter of all offenders facing execution.

There was one great exception to this generally restrained application of the death penalty in colonial America, and it was an exception that echoes today. What made the death penalty most likely in the colonies was not the severity of the offense but the skin color of the offender. African slaves and their descendants were from the very first singled out for indiscriminate and large-scale execution—both to enforce the discipline of slavery and because blacks were considered pagan and resistant to redemption. Between 1706 and 1784, the Virginia colony alone sentenced no fewer than 555 slaves to death. By the late eighteenth century in Connecticut, the only men hanged for sexual assault were black, while whites convicted of the same offense routinely had their sentences commuted. In New York in 1741, some 150 African slaves and 20 whites were accused of plotting an uprising: 30 of the slaves and four whites were executed, with 13 of the slaves burned alive at the stake as an example to other would-be rebels. This just one generation before the American Revolution.

In 1764, a young Italian attorney and economist named Cesar Beccaria almost single-handedly set off the modern crusade against torture and the death penalty by publishing his still-resonant essay "On Crimes and Punishments." "Nothing in the social contract," he proposed, "gives the state the right to take a human life." The death penalty, Beccaria argued, amounts to "a war of the nation against the citizen" that is "neither useful nor necessary." Capital punishment, he wrote, "is ineffectual because of the barbarity of the example it gives to men."

By 1767, Beccaria's writings had been translated into English and were widely read by British and American intellectuals—including many of those who led the American Revolution and would eventually frame the new Constitution. In 1777, Thomas Jefferson proposed abolishing capital punishment in Virginia except for cases of murder and treason; in 1785, such a bill was brought before the Virginia legislature, where it was defeated by only one vote. A few years later, Tom Paine—who had grown up in the English town of Thetford literally within sight of the local gallows—would urge not only the new United States but also revolutionary France to "abolish the penalty of death," and the crusading Irish barrister Daniel O'Connell made the same argument in England.

Shortly after the Revolutionary War ended, Quakers in Pennsylvania founded the Philadelphia Society for Alleviating the Miseries of Public Prisons. One of its leaders, physician Benjamin Rush, a signatory of the Declaration of Independence, gave a lecture at the home of Benjamin Franklin in 1787 entitled "An

Enquiry into the Effects of Public Punishments upon Criminals and upon Society." In that essay and a second treatise published in 1792, Rush expanded on Beccaria with the first reasoned argument in America favoring the abolition of the death penalty, which he called an "absurd and unchristian practice." Rush combined an Enlightenment appeal to reason with Christian religious sentiment: "the obligations of Christianity upon individuals, to promote repentence, to forgive injuries, and to discharge the duties of universal benevolence, are equally binding upon states.

So intense was the debate over capital punishment in Pennsylvania in the ensuing years that pro–death penalty legislators introduced a new distinction—between first- and second-degree murder—greatly narrowing the numbers of the condemned, as a way of keeping capital punishment on the books. William Bradford, the Pennsylvania (and later U.S.) attorney general, argued successfully to limit the death penalty to the most severe cases. In 1794, he persuaded the Pennsylvania legislature to restrict capital punishment even further, to premeditated murder.

The Philadelphia Society became the center of the criminal-justice reform movement throughout the country. In 1808, the Quakers helped establish the first association dedicated to abolishing the death penalty. The first decades of the nineteenth century were marked by the slow but persistent growth of this abolition movement's influence. In 1825, Louisiana nearly passed a criminal code that would have banned capital punishment outright.

By the 1830s, the campaign to abolish or restrict capital punishment had gained undeniable momentum, even as crowds of 30,000 or more would sometimes assemble for hangings. Nearly every state had an anti-gallows society. New York's Mayor Daniel Tompkins took up the cause; by 1832, the New York State Assembly named a committee to "inquire into the expediency" of the abolition of hanging. The committee proposed that the death penalty be virtually eliminated. Its proposals were narrowly defeated in 1834; a year later, the legislature outlawed public hangings, confining executions to prison yards before prescribed witnesses.

In the 1840s, anti-gallows societies and activists—some religious, some secular—were a bona fide political force in several states, pushing not only for an outright end to the death penalty but also for the further narrowing of capital statutes. Indeed, the universal acceptance of degrees of murder today is largely the result of nineteenth-century compromises between death-penalty abolitionists and politicians who wanted to retain executions for some offenses. Lydia Maria Child—a pioneering antislavery journalist and suffragist—campaigned against public executions. The towering antislavery editor and orator Frederick Douglass took up the death-penalty cause, penning an influential pamphlet entitled *Capital Punishment Is a Mockery of Justice.*

The first great triumph for death-penalty opponents, in fact, came more than 100 years before the 1960s. In 1847, Michigan's legislature outright repealed its death penalty for murder. By the mid-1850s Rhode Island and Wisconsin had also done away with capital punishment.

It was only the Civil War—with its 600,000 dead—that stalled the abolition campaign. As historian David Brion Davis of Yale University writes, "Men's finer sensibilities, which once had been revolted by the execution of a fellow human being, seemed hardened and blunted."

But by the late 1800s, the anti-gallows campaign had resumed and gained substantive victories. Kansas, Iowa, and Colorado experimented with doing away with the death penalty. State legislatures vacillated between reason on one hand and the passions of their constituents on the other. Reason would persuade them to outlaw capital punishment; then a heinous crime would drive public debate and the death penalty would be reinstated. Through the same era, some regional differences in death-penalty culture began to emerge, with frontier states like Texas and Wyoming prescribing execution as the penalty for cattle rustling and other offenses. Yet by World War I, 13 states, from Tennessee and Missouri to Maine, had fully or virtually eliminated capital punishment—with Maine, Iowa, and Oregon each abolishing capital punishment twice in successive waves of reform and reaction. In contrast to the death-penalty reforms of the 1960s, this was not abolition by judicial decree; it was state legislatures, backed by popular will.

In fact, in both scale and bureaucratic character, capital punishment as we know it today is entirely a twentieth-century invention—a chilly marriage of technology and politics, beginning with Kemmler's execution in Auburn. Suddenly, the supposedly merciful electric chair was all the rage, and seemed to inspire a new wave of political hunger for execution. By 1920, several of the states that had repealed the death penalty had restored it, and an unprecedented wave of executions began. Perhaps not so coincidentally, this turn-of-the-century resurgence in the death penalty roughly coincided with the great wave of lynchings of African-Americans throughout the South—"unofficial" executions running parallel to those sanctioned by courts.

Bureaucratic, technological, media-driven, the American death penalty is as much a twentieth-century artifact as the auto assembly line or the Zyklon B gas of Auschwitz (a refined version of the cyanide tablets first developed for the Nevada gas chamber in 1924). Scholars at the University of Alabama have assembled a grimly fascinating database of all known executions in the colonies and the United States since George Kendall's hanging in Jamestown in 1608. It is deeply revealing of the varied pace of capital punishment through the years, and during this century in particular. For all the legends of nineteenth-century frontier justice, for instance, it turns out that nationally the number of executions in the 1920s exceeded by a wide margin those of just a few years earlier. In such classic "wild west" states as Wyoming and Utah, executions from 1900 to 1935 were double those of the frontier decades between 1866 and 1899. Executions doubled in Virginia, too. And despite the assumption that the Deep South and Far West are America's historic execution capitals, in the early decades of the twentieth century it was New York, Ohio, and Pennsylvania that led the pack, executions virtually quadrupling in each state to levels unmatched anywhere else in the United States—more than 400 executions in each between 1900 and 1935. The national wave of execution unleashed by New York's electric chair and later the gas chamber peaked in 1935, a year that brought 199 executions nationwide.

The early twentieth century's increasing turn to execution ultimately inspired one of the most influential spokespersons for the abolitionist cause, Unitarian-turned-agnostic lawyer Clarence Darrow. Champion of despised people and unpopular causes, Darrow found both themes coming together in his work as a defense attorney and as an advocate for the abolition of the death penalty. His final murder trial, the 1924 defense of Richard Loeb and Nathan Leopold, who had confessed to the murder of a young boy named Bobby Franks in Chicago, led to their receiving life imprisonment rather than death.

Darrow believed in social determinism: Humans turned to crime because society made them that way, not because of their own free will. He argued that the Civil War and World War I each unleashed a tidal wave of crime: "Do you think that children of our schools and our Sunday schools could be taught killing and be as kindly and tender after it as before?" He believed correctional institutions should be modeled along the lines of hospitals and schools rather than traditional jails or prisons. And he rejected capital punishment because "it is too horrible a thing for the state to undertake. . . . I would hate to live in a state I didn't think was better than a murderer."

The Leopold and Loeb case seemed to revitalize the flagging abolitionist movement. In 1925, the League for the Abolition of Capital Punishment was formed in New York, and in February 1926 it launched its national campaign in New York City just 24 hours before Darrow addressed Congress on the issue. The efforts of the league were further spurred by the case of Nicola Sacco and Bartolomeo Vanzetti, Italian immigrants and anarchists condemned for killing two men in a Lynn, Massachusetts, robbery. Some of the leading legal thinkers of the era believed Sacco and Vanzetti innocent—among them Felix Frankfurter of Harvard, later a Supreme Court justice. Their 1927 execution led to the formation of the Massachusetts Council for the Abolition of the Death Penalty.

Public sentiment continued to seesaw between abolition and retention of the death penalty. Proponents of capital punishment were emboldened by the kidnapping and subsequent murder of the son of legendary flier (and private anti-Semite) Charles Lindbergh, in New Jersey in 1932. In a case that was shot full of inconsistencies, unprofessional actions by the prosecution and the defense, and media sensationalism, Bruno Richard Hauptmann was convicted of the crime and electrocuted in 1936. In response to the public outrage over the crime, the federal government passed what was popularly known as the Lindbergh Act, which made kidnapping a federal crime. The act authorized capital punishment if the victim was not liberated unharmed.

Then, in 1948, the case of Caryl Chessman broke onto the public stage. Chessman was accused of kidnapping and sexual assault in the course of a California robbery. None of the actions of which he was accused were by themselves capital crimes, but a zealous prosectuor charged that together they fell under California's equivalent of the Lindbergh kidnapping-and-bodily-injury law. Chessman, acting as his own lawyer, was found guilty and handed two death sentences. In San Quentin, Chessman taught himself the law, filed his own appeals over 12 years, and eventually presented his case before the U.S. Supreme Court on four different occasions. He wrote four books—one of them a best-seller— and two films were made about his life. Increasingly, the public came to see Chessman as either innocent or disproportionately sentenced to death. California governor Pat Brown tried in vain to convince the California legislature to impose a capital-punishment moratorium in order to forestall Chessman's execution. Chessman's story reignited public debate about capital punishment and brought the first large religious denominations into the fray. From 1956 through the 1980s, a majority of the Protestant and Roman Catholic religious bodies in the United States and Canada took positions in opposition to capital punishment.

In 1958—more than a decade before the U.S. Supreme Court would briefly declare capital punishment unconstitutional—the Delaware state legislature repealed the state's death penalty; legislatures in West Virginia and Iowa soon followed. A public referendum in Oregon abolished the death penalty there in 1964. By that time, executions nationally had fallen from the 1935 high of 199 to just 15; by 1967, the number fell to two, the last executions for a decade.

It was against this backdrop that, in the 1950s and 1960s, the NAACP Legal Defense and Education Fund undertook a series of cases in hopes of halting executions altogether. After a series of Supreme Court rulings in the early 1960s restricting some of the most abusive capital trial practices, in 1966 the LDF initiated a direct assault on the death penalty in the courts, arguing that capital punishment violated the Constitution's Eighth Amendment ban on cruel and unusual punishment and marshaling vast sociological data to show its inequity. The culmination of the LDF's campaign came when, in 1972, the Supreme Court decided the case of *Furman* v. *Georgia*—and by a 5–4 margin found the death penalty as then practiced rife with discrimination, making it an unconstitutionally cruel and arbitrary punishment. So fragmented was the Supreme Court that the nine justices wrote nine different opinions. Justice William O. Douglas described capital punishment as "pregnant with discrimination." Justice Byron White called it "pointless and needless."

In the polarized political climate of the early 1970s, reaction to *Furman* among some politicians was immediate and violent. Georgia's Governor Lester Maddox called the decision "a license for anarchy, rape and murder." California's then-Governor Ronald Reagan called for reviving the death penalty using lethal injections. Legal conservatives—who had also long opposed the Supreme Court's intervention in desegregation and in the rights of criminal defendants—saw in this reaction an opportunity to swing the Court in a new direction, taking advantage of the retirement of older justices.

After just four years, with *Gregg* v. *Georgia* in 1976, the Supreme

Court changed course in a 7–2 decision finding that "the punishment of death does not invariably violate the Constitution." The political reaction to *Furman,* said Justice Lewis Powell for the Court's majority, proves that "a large proportion of American society continues to regard [capital punishment] as an appropriate and necessary criminal sanction." In *Gregg* and cases that followed, the new pro-execution majority on the Court set down new rules for executions supposedly designed to prevent arbitrary justice or discrimination and requiring jurors or judges in the states to weigh "aggravating" and "mitigating" factors in any death case. *Gregg* made the United States the first—and still the only—country to reintroduce capital punishment after its abolition.

In effect, the years after 1967 had marked the first national moratorium on capital punishment, a moratorium broken in theory by *Gregg* and in practice with Gary Gilmore's execution by firing squad in Utah in 1977. The same year marked the beginning of a new death-penalty era in another way as well: Oklahoma became the first state to approve execution by lethal injection on the grounds that it would be less costly than "Old Sparky." The quarter century since has been marked by an ever escalating number of executions, today rivaling the all-time high of the 1930s even as new doubts and questions are sweeping the public.

If early America distinguished itself from England with its relative reluctance to embrace execution, today's execution-frantic America finds itself increasingly isolated on the world stage. After years of debate over whether execution could be made more humane, Britain's Parliament abolished capital punishment in 1969. Sweden and Spain abolished the death penalty in 1972 and 1975 respectively. In 1981 France abolished the guillotine after a long campaign led by Senator Robert Badinter (today a leading European voice against U.S. capital punishment). In 1989 UNESCO ruled that the death penalty should not be used for mentally retarded individuals. In 1990 the United Nations called on all member nations to take steps toward abolishing capital punishment. Switzerland outlawed capital punishment in 1992, and our neighbors Canada and Mexico have also abolished the practice. In 1995 South Africa abolished it as well. Pope John Paul II has called upon the United States to cease executions, and in 2000 the European Union voted to refuse to extradite accused murderers to any country where they might be executed—in other words, to the United States. Today the United States remains the only Western industrialized nation that executes its citizens.

Capital punishment has never been absent from America's political geography. Yet history shows that, far from being an inevitable part of the nation's culture, capital punishment has been contentious and contended ground since the beginning; and far from being a constant of criminal law, capital punishment has instead ebbed and flowed, a tool of the politics of race and the politics of crime rather than of enduring national principles. Today, the politics of capital punishment are once again in flux, the pendulum swinging away from the unprecedented waves of state-sponsored bloodshed that marked the previous American century.

CHAPTER 2

Myths, Lies, and

Deterrence

In the close and contentious presidential campaign of 2000, candidates Al Gore and George W. Bush didn't agree on much. They fought over taxes, over education, over affirmative action, over oil drilling.

But one curious point of agreement emerged in the final presidential debate, on October 19, 2000. It was not a reporter who asked the revealing question but an audience member, Leo Anderson. Mr. Anderson pointed out how in a debate one week earlier, Governor Bush seemed to "overly enjoy" invoking the death penalty during a discussion of hate crimes and the murder of James Byrd, an African-American man dragged to death in Texas. "Are you really, really proud of the fact that Texas is number one in executions?" Anderson asked.

Well, no, replied the Texas governor. "If you think I was proud of it, I think you misread me." But then he added: "I think the reason to support the death penalty is because it saves other people's lives." Gore, clearly not wanting to be outdone in the law-and-order department, chimed in with the same assertion: "It's a deterrence."

"It saves other people's lives." "It's a deterrence." Those simple phrases, articulated by two presidential candidates across wide gulfs of party and philosophy, express the most commonly held view of capital punishment's value. Killing killers prevents crime. The death penalty makes a safer society.

There is only one problem with this logic: It isn't true.

Whatever the philosophical justifications might be for capital punishment, deterring crime isn't among them. Just ask the nation's top law enforcement officials. A 1995 poll by Hart Research Associates found that just 1 percent of the nation's police chiefs believe the death penalty significantly reduces the number of homicides. Then–Attorney General Janet Reno, a death-penalty supporter whose Justice Department crafted laws making it far harder for death-row inmates to appeal their sentences, put it this way in 1999: "I have inquired for most of my adult life about studies that might show the death penalty is a deterrent. And I have not seen any research that would substantiate that point."

The belief that the severity of execution discourages others from wrongdoing is probably as old as the death penalty itself. As long ago as 1566, Pope Pius V in his Roman Catechism declared that the death penalty, along with other punishments, gives "security to life by repressing outrage and violence." In colonial America, Protestant ministers routinely delivered public sermons on the eve of executions extolling the virtue of hanging's example. In 1790, New Haven, Connecticut, minister James Dana delivered one such sermon—entitled simply "The Aims of Capital Punishment"—three hours before the hanging of James Mountain, a free black man convicted of raping a white teenage girl. The purpose of capital punishment, Dana declared, was both "to rid the state of a present nuisance" and particularly "to strike terror into the minds of undetected criminals, youth and all persons watching." The execution of Mountain would be "a spectacle to the world, a warning to the vicious."

Yet by the time of Dana's sermon, influential voices were already challenging the logic of deterrence, beginning with Beccaria, who declared capital punishment not just morally wrong but "ineffectual." Far from reducing crime, Beccaria argued, execution actually creates it, raising the stakes for lawbreakers, making desperate individuals only more desperate, and setting an example of brutality:

> The worse the ill that confronts them, the more men are driven to evade it. The very savagery of punishment has this effect, and to avoid the penalty for one crime they have already committed, men commit other crimes. Countries and times in which punishments have been the most savage have always been those of the bloodiest and most inhuman acts, inasmuch as the spirit of ferocity which guided the hand of the lawgiver also guided the hand of the parricide and cutthroat.

In 1825, attorney and politician Edward Livingstone—who in a career of astonishing breadth represented both New York and Louisiana in Congress, was elected mayor of New York City, and ultimately appointed secretary of state by Andrew Jackson—proposed a model Louisiana criminal code that completely abolished capital punishment. In terms that sound utterly contemporary to our ears, he challenged his opponents to make their best case:

By your own account, all nations, since the first institution of society, have practiced it, but you yourselves must acknowlege, without success. All we ask, then, is that you abandon an experiment which has for five or six thousand years been progressing under the variety of forms which cruel ingenuity could invent; and which in all ages, under all governments, has been found wanting. . . . You have made your experiment . . . it was found often fatal to the innocent, and it frequently permitted the guilty to escape. . . . Tortures were superadded, which nothing but the intelligence of a fiend could invent; yet there was no diminution of crime.

A few years later, in the 1840s, Robert Rantoul, a Massachusetts state representative, conducted the first systematic study of deterrence and came to the conclusion that it didn't work. He believed that by devaluing human life and sanctioning an official policy of vengeance, the death penalty actually increased the violence in society and, hence, the murder rate.

Rantoul addressed his colleagues in the state legislature in an 1846 debate on public executions, presenting evidence that disputed his opponents' claims of deterrence. He explained that in nations such as England and France, where the proportion of executions to convictions was much smaller than in Massachusetts, and also much smaller than the rate in those countries 50 years before, the murder rate was actually decreasing. He had also studied the murder and execution rates in Belgium and noted that the three years in which there were more than 50 executions a year were followed by the three most murderous years in Belgium's history.

With the advent of social science and modern statistical methods, scholars looked anew at the death-penalty deterrence factor.

Early in the twentieth century, American researchers compared homicide rates in states that had abolished the death penalty to rates in neighboring states that continued to use capital punishment. Five decades of research across the country failed to show a higher murder rate in states that had abolished the death penalty.

A number of researchers also took a look at states that had either abolished the death penalty or had reinstated its use after a period of abolition. In startling contradiction to what deterrence theory predicts, these studies found that murder rates were stable; they did not rise after a state stopped using capital punishment, nor did they decline when a state reintroduced capital punishment. In the late 1950s, sociologist Thorsten Sellin studied five groups of similar states in the Midwest and New England, with each group including at least one state that used the death penalty while the others did not. Sellin found that the average homicide rate in these states between 1940 and 1955 was in no way related to whether or not the state sanctioned execution as a punishment.

Yet by the late 1970s deterrence arguments were making a comeback. The decade from 1967 to 1977 in which no executions were carried out in the United States coincided with a widespread rise in crime; although scholars differed (and still differ) about the reasons for that rise, politicians and policymakers seized upon the death penalty as a panacea for public fear, after *Furman* v. *Georgia* in 1972, rushing through new laws they hoped would meet with Supreme Court approval. Capital punishment was proposed as a deterrent to everything from serial-sexual predators to presidential assassinations.

Against this backdrop, Isaac Ehrlich's 1975 study "The Deterrent Effect of Capital Punishment: A Question of Life and Death" landed like a bombshell. Ehrlich analyzed annual national homicide and execution rates from 1933 until 1970. Using computerized statistical methods and controlling for a number of other factors that contribute to the homicide rate—such as unemployment, age distribution, and per capita income—Ehrlich found a deterrent factor. Based on his numbers, Ehrlich boldly estimated that each execution deterred approximately eight homicides—a figure seized upon immediately by death-penalty advocates.

But in the years that followed, numerous scientists failed to replicate Ehrlich's results, and his methods are now considered profoundly suspect. For example, researchers using an econometric model, a newer and more powerful statistical procedure, concluded that Ehrlich's data did not support his results. Another researcher refined Ehrlich's social and economic controls on poverty, educational levels, and family structures. These refinements appeared to account for the "deterrent factor" that Ehrlich had supposedly found. Still other analysts showed that by lumping together statistics from all of the states, he masked significant differences in rates among states, specifically between states maintaining the death penalty and those that had abolished capital punishment.

Ehrlich's research, in any event, was entirely historical. Utah's execution of Gary Gilmore in 1977 and the growing number of executions that followed inspired a new generation of contemporary research. Psychology professor Sam McFarland saw these first executions as his opportunity to test the claim of death-penalty supporters that the fear of receiving the ultimate sanction deterred would-be criminals from committing murder. The first four executions after reinstitution occurred between 1977 and 1981. McFarland analyzed the weekly homicide rates in the months following these executions and found that in the two weeks following Gilmore's execution, national homicide rates were significantly below average. However, the next three executions had no perceptible effect on the murder rate.

A less thorough researcher might have concluded that the results confirmed a deterrent factor that was dependent on public awareness, but McFarland searched for other factors. He determined that Gilmore's execution coincided with some of the worst winter weather to hit the eastern half of the country in years. Blizzards blanketed the East Coast as far south as Georgia and Alabama, and the mercury plunged far below normal in the January weeks immediately after Gilmore's execution.

When he examined his data regionally, McFarland found a sharp drop in homicides in the Northeast and the South during the exceptionally inclement period, but in western states experiencing normal weather patterns, homicide rates were at their usual levels. Gilmore's execution didn't deter potential killers; several feet of snow and bitter wind chills did.

Larger-scale studies since have deflated even further any claims that capital punishment deters crime. William C. Bailey, a sociologist at Cleveland State University, has scoured crime statistics for evidence that execution discourages crime ever since the mid-1970s. Bailey's work has ranged from the historic (Chicago homicides and executions in the 1920s) to the contemporary (killings of police officers from the 1970s onward). After breaking down figures into every conceivable category from serial killing to domestic violence, and examining homicides that fall short of first-degree murder as well, Bailey reached this conclusion:

> Neither economists nor sociologists, nor persons from any other discipline (law, psychology, engineering, etc.) have

produced credible evidence of a significant deterrent for capital punishment. . . . The evidence remains "clear and abundant" that, as practiced in the United States, capital punishment is not more effective than imprisonment in reducing murder.

Bailey is not alone in his devastating conclusion about the death penalty's irrelevance as a deterrent. In 1999 the scholarly journal *Crime and Delinquency* examined more than a decade of executions in George W. Bush's Texas, and found "no evidence of a deterrent effect." Other research has reached the same conclusion, most notably a 1997 study of crime in more than 500 counties nationwide.

Deterrence theory is predicated on the seemingly commonsense notion that the possibility of receiving the death penalty will deter would-be killers, whereas the possibility of receiving a sentence of life in prison without possibility of parole will not. If murderers were rational people educated in the laws of the states in which they live, the theory might have some weight. For criminals to be deterred by the penalty, they must know the possible penalties in the state in which they commit their crimes and, in addition, must rationally weigh the risks and benefits of their actions.

Most homicides, however, are unplanned, impulsive acts by one person against another. The emotionally charged environment in which these crimes take place does not suggest a cool, calculating murderer weighing his options.

If a murderer were to sit down to calculate the odds of being punished for a premeditated act of violence, this is what he would have to consider. In the United States, the death penalty is handed down for only about 1 out of every 100 homicides. In capital cases, the rate is higher, but it is still only 6 to 15 per 100 offenses (depending on the state), and of those sentenced, only 6 per 100 are executed. With these odds, the threat of being killed by the planned victim or in a confrontation with police is a much more realistic threat than the distant and abstract possibility of execution. But even those more immediate threats have yet to eliminate the violent crime in our streets. A 1980 study by William Bowers and Glenn Pierce titled "Deterrence or Brutalization: What Is the Effect of Executions?" showed that the primary distinguishing characteristic between those imprisoned for homicide and those imprisoned for the lesser charge of aggravated assault was that the victims of the former were unarmed or intoxicated. Neither the killers' intent nor any deterrence by laws played a major part.

In fact, there is only one conceivable "deterrent" in the death penalty: that the person executed is undeniably prevented from committing a crime again. Yet if that narrow kind of "deterrence"—the irrevocable incapacitation of a single offender—is the only goal, incarceration, including, where appropriate, life without parole, provides as much protection for society.

Yet politicians persist in trafficking in the deterrence myth. Some try to turn the failure of the death penalty to deter crime into a reason to pump up the capital-punishment machine even further: "If we're going to have a death penalty on the books, it ought to be a real deterrent," Connecticut's Governor John Rowland said in early 2001, arguing for speeding up executions and imposing the death penalty for more offenses.

At times, the deterrence myth bleeds over into outright lies or fantasy. In that October 2000 presidential debate, George W. Bush declared his capital-punishment apparatus in Texas part of a successful crime-fighting machine: "I'm proud of the fact that violent crime is down in the state of Texas. I'm proud of the fact that we hold people accountable."

Bush's crime-fighting success, unfortunately, is a figment of his imagination. According to figures in the FBI's Uniform Crime Reports released in the same month as the Bush-Gore debate, while crime is declining in cities nationwide, it is rising in the large cities of Texas. The FBI's figures confirm a study by the Justice Police Institute of Washington, D.C., which found crime falling more slowly in Bush's Texas than in any comparable state. The only other state to defy the national crime drop is Florida, which is also the only state to rival Texas in the pace of executions. By comparison New York, which although it has reinstated the death penalty has not actually executed anyone in decades, leads the nation's most populous states in driving crime downward.

Why, then, does the deterrence myth persist? Police know the death penalty doesn't deter crime. Crime-policy experts know it. The scholars know it. It is only politicians, it seems, who have not heard the news.

CHAPTER 3

Sleeping Lawyer Syndrome

and Other Tales of Justice for the Poor

"The Constitution says that everyone's entitled to an attorney of their choice. But the Constitution does not say that the lawyer has to be awake."
—JUDGE DOUG SHAVER, TEXAS DISTRICT COURT

"Them's that got the capital don't get the punishment."

—MUMIA ABU-JAMAL

A few years ago, Judge Alex Kozinski of the U.S. Court of Appeals for the Ninth Circuit wrote in *The New Yorker* of the insomnia he suffers when he sends a death-row defendant to execution. But he goes through with it thanks to his confidence that today's capital cases are "meticulously litigated."

Judge Kozinski was voicing a commonly held opinion, an opinion supported by several decades of tough-on-crime rhetoric from politicians. But anyone seeking to reality-test Judge Kozinski's assertion need look no further than the case of George McFarland of Houston, whose petition for an expedited review by the U.S. Supreme Court was turned down just a week after Kozinski published his article in 1996. McFarland was sentenced to death in Houston in August 1992 for killing Kenneth Kwan, a convenience store owner. Judge Kozinski could read the McFarland trial transcript without disrupting his own docket; the case moved with bullet-train velocity. Opening statements on August 10, 1992; guilty verdict on August 12; death sentence on August 14. With lunch and the occasional recess, it required not more than 16 hours of "meticulous litigation" for Texas to transform George McFarland from Presumed Innocent into Dead Man Walking.

Even a cursory reading of that "meticulous" trial record is enough to suggest that Texas sent McFarland—a 35-year-old petty thief—hurtling toward execution on the basis of evidence that in many states wouldn't make a parking ticket stick. But the most startling fact of McFarland's trial was not recorded in the transcript. It involved not McFarland but his lawyer, one John Benn. Here's how the *Houston Chronicle* described what happened as McFarland stood on trial for his life:

> Seated beside his client . . . defense attorney John Benn spent much of Thursday afternoon's trial in apparent deep sleep.
>
> His mouth kept falling open and his head lolled back on his shoulders, and then he awakened just long enough to catch himself and sit upright. Then it happened again. And again. And again.
>
> Every time he opened his eyes, a different prosecution witness was on the stand describing another aspect of the

November 19, 1991, arrest of George McFarland in the rob-
bery-killing of grocer Kenneth Kwan.

When state District judge Doug Shaver finally called a recess, Benn was asked if he truly had fallen asleep during a capital murder trial.

"It's boring," the 72-year-old longtime Houston lawyer explained. . . .

Court observers said Benn seems to have slept his way
through virtually the entire trial.

The idea of a lawyer sleeping through a murder trial is a little
disconcerting. Unless you are from Texas, where sleeping-lawyer
capital cases are a bona fide trend. In recent years the Texas Court
of Appeals (the state's highest court) has turned down three peti-
tions from death-row inmates whose lawyers slept through significant parts of their trials. And the U.S. Court of Appeals for the
Eleventh Circuit has in at least one recent case let a Texas sleeping-
lawyer death sentence stand.

A death sentence always gives the phrase "right to counsel" a
special edge. The fact that Americans accused of crime have any
right to a lawyer can be traced back to 1932, when seven young
black men in Scottsboro, Alabama, were sentenced to death for
rape under questionable circumstances. After reviewing the
abysmal work of the two lawyers who represented these men and
the hostility in the community surrounding the case, the Supreme
Court ruled that the defendants "did not have the aid of counsel in
any real sense." In *Powell* v. *Alabama,* the Court established the
precedent that any person facing capital punishment who is too
poor to afford an attorney has the right to have an attorney assigned to him.

It was not until 30 years later, during the Kennedy administration, that all the people of the United States received the right to appointed counsel in any felony case if they could not afford one. The Supreme Court would not have made this ruling if it hadn't decided to accept a handwritten petition from Clarence Earl Gideon, a prisoner in Florida. Although Gideon was poor, he understood the Sixth Amendment: "In all criminal prosecutions, the accused shall . . . have the right of counsel for his defense." It took this nation 174 years to make that promise in the Constitution available to indigent criminal defendants.

Yet from the moment the Supreme Court reinstated capital punishment in 1976, one question has haunted death-row cases: How awful must a lawyer be before the right to counsel is violated in such cases? That's been a critical and unresolved question—especially in the South, because of the number of defendants sentenced to death there and because of the horrifically low fees allocated to death-row lawyers in many southern states. In Kentucky, court-appointed defense lawyers are paid $2,500 for an entire trial; in Mississippi, an average of $11.75 per hour.

That same question—Just what is the threshold of incompetence?—was percolating constantly through the courts of Texas in early 1992, when George McFarland was arrested for the murder some weeks earlier of Kenneth Kwan, a Korean immigrant. How McFarland's case played out shows in minute particulars the stakes in "poor man's justice." On November 19, 1991, Kwan arrived at his Houston convenience store from the bank. He was carrying a sack of money to cash customers' paychecks. He had driven back from the bank with James Powell, a shotgun-bearing security guard; Ken Kwan's wife waited inside the store. As they drove up, a man stood on the sidewalk with a plastic bag of clothing, as if going to the laundromat next door. Suddenly the man with the bag pulled out a pistol, put it to Powell's head, and told him to drop the shotgun. Powell dropped it. Another man appeared on the scene. Someone—it is not clear who, or even how many guns were involved—fired at Kwan, who was shot five times in the chest and back. The second man grabbed Kwan's sack of cash and the two vanished in a car. A customer named Carolyn Bartie who was driving up as the robbery started helped Mrs. Kwan pull her husband into the store. Kwan got to the hospital at noon and was dead two hours later.

For weeks, the police had no suspects. Neither the security guard Powell nor the customer Bartie gave a specific description of Kwan's killer, except that he was an African-American around six feet in height. Both doubted they would ever recognize him. Their stories of what happened, and which man had fired on Kwan, differed radically. There was no physical evidence, no other witnesses.

More than a month after the murder, a phone call came to Crime Stoppers, a public informant line. A young man named Craig Burks offered to finger his uncle, George McFarland—a three-time loser who had done time for a $1,200 jewelry heist, a mugging, and car theft. McFarland, Burks said, had taken him for a drive around the time of Kwan's shooting and flashed a roll of bills. Then, said Burks, Uncle George boasted of taking part in the robbery and named two other buddies as well, though he said he had nothing to do with the murder.

Burks was not exactly an ideal witness. He had a history of mental illness and prolonged hospitalization. He had several times tried to drop the dime on others through Crime Stoppers in hope of collecting the line's standard $900 reward, and his tips had always turned out to be a hustle. Finally, Craig Burks had only recently pleaded guilty to an aggravated robbery charge of his own and was facing prison. He'd testify against McFarland if in addition to collecting the $900 reward the charge against him was reduced and jail time dropped.

The Houston District Attorney's office agreed to Burks' demand and brought George McFarland in. The security guard, Powell, however—who had stood next to the robber—couldn't identify him. The customer, Carolyn Bartie, who at the time of Kwan's killing swore she would never be able to identify the killer, and who it turned out was a civilian employee of the police department working downstairs from the homicide squad, said McFarland might be the man who held Powell at gunpoint, but she couldn't be sure from the photo lineup she was shown. It was only after she studied McFarland's photo—effectively, putting his image into her head—and then was shown him in a live lineup that she decided that this was the man she had seen.

Thus a purchased statement from an unstable informant and a coached witness identification were the full extent of evidence against George McFarland when he went to trial in August of 1992.

It's easy to imagine how a well-paid defense lawyer, a Johnnie Cochrane or an F. Lee Bailey, might have disposed of such a case. But McFarland's family hired Benn, a low-rent fixture in Houston's courts for 42 years. Judge Shaver later described him as "a little long in the tooth." In fact, when the case hit Shaver's docket, he took one look at the somnambulant Benn and without even asking McFarland appointed a second, presumably more vigorous lawyer to assist, a self-employed defense attorney named Sandy Melamed, who would be paid the minimal compensation offered by Texas' courts.

Court records suggest that the two lawyers were a dream team only in the most unintended sense. Melamed testified during McFarland's appeal that when Judge Shaver appointed him, "I called

[Benn] at his office and asked if he wanted to have a discussion about who would do what. He did not." In fact neither lawyer did much to prepare for McFarland's murder trial. Benn, the lead counsel, met with McFarland just once in the lockup. Melamed testified that he spent "five, six, seven hours" preparing for this death-penalty trial. The lawyers arranged no investigation, and they made no attempt to locate the other suspects fingered by Burks or potential witnesses whose names McFarland provided. Between them, Benn and Melamed spent fewer than two work days preparing for a trial that would determine whether George McFarland would live or die.

Benn later admitted that he and Melamed did not compare notes during the trial, not even to prepare for final arguments. As for Benn's sleeping—"I customarily take a short nap in the afternoon" was his only explanation. Melamed later said he thought Benn's sleeping might "make the jury feel sorry for us."

Now, a reasonable person might decide that this Sleepy-Dopey tag team hardly constituted effective assistance of counsel; and that lead counsel Benn's state of consciousness might have made a difference in a death-penalty case with such slim evidence. In the words of one federal appeals court, "sleeping counsel is the equivalent to no counsel at all."

But this is Texas. In Texas, one judge after another has found that sleeping lawyers are no barrier to a fair death-penalty trial. In 1995 the state executed Carl Johnson, whose trial lawyer Joe Cannon had in the words of Johnson's appeal "slept during jury selection and parts of the defense itself" and was later disciplined for incompetence in another death-row case. No surprise, then, that in February 1996 the Texas Court of Appeals by a 7–2 margin agreed that the sleeping John Benn was no reason to reopen McFarland's conviction or reconsider his death sentence. During

McFarland's trial Judge Doug Shaver responded to attorney Benn's unconscious-at-the-bar behavior with the memorable bit of constitutional philosophy that opens this chapter.

Any reasonable person would conclude that George McFarland, like the Scottsboro Boys decades earlier, "did not have the aid of counsel in any real sense." And whether or not McFarland—at this writing still on death row—is a killer is literally impossible to know from his trial. Yet the U.S. Supreme Court, evidently, doesn't see any of this as a problem, since it has yet to hear a sleeping-lawyer appeal and declined to grant George McFarland an expedited hearing.

But that is precisely the point. As George McFarland's case illustrates, the facts are simple: Inadequate lawyering, outright bad lawyering, is at the heart of capital punishment in America. The death penalty is imposed not for the worst crime but for the worst lawyer—and that outcome is usually a matter of economics.

Traditionally, defense lawyers have fought the death penalty on issues of legal principle while sparing the cynics and incompetents in their profession much scrutiny. But Stephen S. Bright of the Southern Center for Human Rights in Atlanta has meticulously documented dozens of hair-raising cases involving both court-appointed and privately hired death-penalty trial lawyers: lawyers who showed up at trial raving drunk, lawyers who called their clients "little nigger boy," lawyers who couldn't recite a single criminal statute or case. "It is not the facts of the case but the quality of representation" that determines whether a defendant ends up on death row, Bright's research reveals. He is not alone in his conclusion. The widely respected *National Law Journal* studied capital cases in six southern states and turned up a parade of "ill trained, ill prepared . . . grossly underpaid" death-penalty lawyers. Whether or not a defendant ends up with a death sentence, the

Law Journal found, is "more like a random flip of the coin than a delicate balancing of the scales."

Red flags concerning the woeful lack of representation accorded capital criminals have been raised by a number of Supreme Court justices, including Thurgood Marshall, William Brennan, and Harry Blackmun. Even Justice Sandra Day O'Connor has said, "There's probably never been a wider gulf between the need for legal services and the provision of those services. There is a great deal to be concerned about, or even ashamed of."

Yet the crisis in capital representation persists. While highly qualified lawyers have often represented death-row inmates on appeal for no fee—in many cases freeing utterly innocent individuals—it is at the trial level where the real damage occurs, and it always—always—involves the poorest defendants. "Virtually all men and women on death row are and were poor," notes veteran Florida capital-appeals attorney Michael Mello, now a professor at Vermont Law School. "Most had lousy lawyering and investigating at the trial level. Cops and prosecutors still hide evidence of innocence from capital defendants and their attorneys"—evidence that the paltry investigative resources provided to indigent attorneys cannot possibly turn up.

Indeed, in recent years the crisis has only worsened. Until recently, death-row defendants could at least count on federally funded legal aid bureaus—so-called death-penalty resource centers—to sustain their appeals. But in 1996 Congress pulled the financial plug on the death-row resource centers, effectively stranding inmates without representation or investigative resources.

To understand what it meant for Congress to end this program, consider the case of Lloyd Schlup. Schlup was accused of a murder that took place while he was incarcerated for another crime.

43

Unlike the daily visits by Robert Shapiro to O. J. Simpson, Schlup's trial attorney visited him twice for a total of 75 minutes before trial. They never talked on the phone. Despite his failure to interview any of the 20 witnesses who saw the murder, the attorney was paid $2,000 for representation. Schlup's 1985 murder trial took two days, and he was convicted. Eventually, Schlup came within an hour of his execution.

It was the Missouri Resource Center that came to Schlup's aid, working with a new appeals lawyer who agreed to take on the case for no fee. Schlup's new lawyers turned up an enormous amount of evidence of innocence, including a videotape and those 20 eyewitnesses proving that he was nowhere near the scene of the crime. So compelling was the new evidence that finally Missouri's governor, Mel Carnahan, agreed to halt his execution and review the case for possible clemency. Ultimately, in 1995, a narrow majority of the U.S. Supreme Court agreed that the evidence demanded a new trial. Schlup, fearful of a second death sentence, finally pleaded guilty to a lesser charge. Had Schlup sought help after 1996, there would have been no Resource Center. He would have been out of luck—and most likely dead.

A dramatic and graphic example of the erosion of death-row representation can be seen in the courts of Philadelphia, Pennsylvania. In the birthplace of American liberty, justice is becoming ever more simply another commodity available only to the few who can afford it; when resources are scarce, the constitutional protections that distinguish our system of government are the first to be jettisoned.

According to a 1991 survey by the National Association of Counties, fully 40 percent of counties in the country with populations exceeding 100,000 face major budgetary shortfalls. All of them have been forced to trim away resources required for equal justice to prevail. At the top of the list of resource-strapped counties is Philadelphia. As already inadequate funding for indigent defense programs has been slashed across the nation, Pennsylvania provides no funds at all for such defense. Philadelphia itself has no organized system to provide training or support for attorneys who defend capital cases, and the public defender system, which in 1991 was finally empowered to take on up to 20 percent of indigent capital cases, has no funding for that responsibility and has had no cases assigned to it.

As of January 2001, 243 people were under sentence of death in the Commonwealth of Pennsylvania. With less than 15 percent of the state's population, Philadelphia accounts for more than half of the state's condemned prisoners. One reason for this is that the Philadelphia district attorney's office seeks the death penalty in well over 50 percent of all homicides, or about 300 cases a year. This requires defense counsel to prepare to defend against a capital charge, even though it may be unwarranted by the facts.

Only about 80 lawyers out of approximately 8,000 in the city both qualify and are willing to represent capitally charged defendants. Since most of the defendants are poor, to undertake such cases is to agree to work for little remuneration. Court-appointed lawyers are forced to wait up to two years between the time they are appointed and when they can collect their fees. They cannot even request payment until after the sentence has been affirmed by the court, a process that usually takes about 14 months. After filing for fees ($40 an hour for out-of-court time and $50 for in-court, a fraction of what a competent Philadelphia attorney can bill a private client), not only do they have to wait up to another year to be paid, their billable time is often cut. As one respected defense attorney describes it, "We extend credit to the city for two years, so it's no wonder that most lawyers just process cases."

When compensation is both insufficient and belated, experienced death-penalty lawyers become extremely reluctant to take new capital cases. They know the amount of time necessary to prepare and present a decent defense. "A system being held together on the backs of counsel having to beg and borrow is guaranteed to provide second-rate representation," says experienced Philadelphia trial lawyer Samuel Stretton. "The best lawyers don't do them anymore."

While it may be hard to summon sympathy for attorneys, the real victims of such a system are the very rights and protections we take for granted as distinguishing our form of government. Ironically, when these protections are sacrificed in the interests of cost and expediency, much larger expenditures of resources are implicated down the line.

In testimony on behalf of the American Bar Association, Columbia University law professor James S. Liebman reported to Congress on the findings of the ABA Task Force on Death Penalty Habeas Corpus. The report noted that poor compensation almost inevitably means that only inexperienced and ill-prepared lawyers will be available to handle capital cases, and that lawyers will not develop expertise because they will be financially unable to handle more than one capital case. Not surprisingly, therefore, the inexperienced and inexpert counsel who handle many of the cases frequently conduct inadequate factual investigations, are unable to keep abreast of the complex and constantly changing legal doctrines that apply in capital litigation, and mistakenly fail to make timely objections to improper procedures.

As Professor Liebman explained to Congress, the findings of the ABA task force show that "the high level of constitutional error implanted in capital trials and appeals by uncompensated, inexpert, and ill-prepared counsel has required the federal courts to overturn and order retrials of more than 40 percent of the post-1976 death sentences that they have reviewed. . . . Moreover, the expensive and time-consuming proceedings necessary to uncover that astonishing number of constitutional violations and to retry and review all those cases is without doubt the single largest cause of delay in capital litigation."

The impact is stunningly visible in Philadelphia. As Judge William Manfredi, the homicide calendar judge who determines the initial allocation of resources in death-penalty trials, says, "Eighty competent attorneys out of eight thousand attorneys is outrageous." And at the same time, while the pool of qualified defense counsel grows smaller, the number of cases the district attorney prosecutes capitally grows larger, further stretching the system. Indeed, many Philadelphia lawyers identify the DA's practice of overcharging in homicide cases as among the most pernicious aspects of Philadelphia's death-penalty process.

Judge Manfredi describes the judges' job as balancing "the competing interests of quality representation with the economic situation of Philadelphia." For the families of poor, capitally charged defendants—the death penalty seems reserved exclusively for the poor—this balancing act allows them only to watch helplessly as their loved ones face the possibility of execution without the assistance of the experts we would all demand for ourselves or our loved ones in similar circumstances.

Anthony Reid was such a defendant. Abandoned by his parents before his first birthday and raised in poverty with seven foster brothers and sisters, Reid was charged with homicide at the age of 20. He was unable to afford counsel, and so the court appointed Samuel Stretton.

At the beginning of Reid's trial, Stretton asked that his client be examined by a psychologist, who might uncover facets of Reid's life that could help the jury get a more complete picture of the young man. Presiding Judge Albert Sabo—who, before his retirement, sent more defendants to death row than any judge in America, and is most famous as the judge in Mumia Abu-Jamal's trial—denied the motion on the grounds that it was an unwarranted expense, at least until Reid was convicted and the jury needed to determine his appropriate sentence.

On January 9, 1991, Reid was convicted. The next day, the penalty phase began, and Stretton renewed his request for a psychological evaluation and testimony. "Your client told me . . . that he has no problems at all, so what are we going to look for?" Judge Sabo asked the startled defense attorney.

Dr. Gerald Cook, an experienced forensic psychologist, was in the courtroom at Stretton's request, ready and willing to conduct the examination of Reid.

"I want the jury to understand his personality . . . his intellect. . . . I am looking for mitigating circumstances," Stretton said.

"Why don't you dig for gold while you're at it?" Sabo interrupted.

Before ruling on Stretton's request for the expert witness, Sabo turned to the prosecuting attorney and asked his opinion. Like the judge, he too relied on the "expertise" of the 22-year-old Reid himself, who swore "under oath that he has no psychological problems."

Stretton protested. "I have retained a psychologist."

"Take care of it out of your fee," the judge replied, sarcastically. "There is no basis for me to expend public funds needlessly."

"I am court-appointed," the defense attorney protested one last time. "There is a good chance we will never be paid. . . ."

"A good chance he [the psychologist] would never be paid, either," Judge Sabo said, dismissing the request.

Thus, in the crucial penalty phase, during which the defendant is allowed to provide any information for the jury to consider in mitigation of the sentence, the jury heard only the predictable pleas for mercy of Mr. Reid's foster sisters, begging for his life. "I am just asking for his life, just don't take his life," Lydia Banks begged. "He's only 22. He can change. He's suffering. Our family are all suffering. . . . I'm just asking for you not to take his physical life!"

Lydia Banks ran out of the courtroom, weeping. Another sister, also hysterical, was ordered removed. Without the benefit or guidance of a professional evaluation, with no expert psychological testimony to assess, the jury sentenced Reid to die by lethal injection.

The problem is made worse by its unpredictability. "I always grant money for experts," says Philadelphia criminal-court judge David Savitt. But he admits that other judges routinely deny such requests. Because there is no institutional system governing either the request or the response, both the quality of defense and the outcome are widely divergent.

As Reid's case shows, the crisis in capital representation isn't just a matter of lawyers' fees. It is also about basic investigation. Ironically, just as Congress was cutting death-penalty resource centers, new DNA tests and other scientific tools were becoming available to prove—in completely objective fashion—the innocence or guilt of some inmates. But DNA testing is costly. Although New York and Illinois have passed model legislation guaranteeing every defendant the right to postconviction DNA testing, in most states indigent defendants and their court-appointed lawyers are left to fend for themselves. (At this writing, Senator Patrick Leahy's Innocence Protection Act, which would provide funding to support DNA testing and other protections, languishes in Congress.)

So serious is the financial squeeze on investigation and expert testimony in death cases that many experts simply no longer provide their services to the defense, because they feel they cannot play a responsible role. Dr. Robert Sadoff will no longer serve as an expert for the defense in court-appointed cases in Philadelphia—though he continues to testify in New Jersey, Ohio, Alabama, and Mississippi—because he cannot rely on promises of payment down the road. "I'm standing on the sidelines until a reliable and fair fee schedule, paid on time, is a regular part of the system," he says.

With so much evidence of imbalance and injustice in the system, why does the crisis of capital representation—the death penalty for the worst lawyer—still persist and indeed accelerate? In large part because, nationwide, elected prosecutors, judges, and legislators have fought even token reforms in the capital-representation system. The fact is that for ambitious elected district attorneys and judges, death-penalty cases are high-profile opportunities. They know that stronger lawyers for inmates on trial for their lives means fewer convictions and death sentences, fewer notches on their prosecutorial belts to wave in the face of voters. Better capital representation means greater exposure of false confessions, bungled police work, and other abuses.

The irony is that the shocking state of capital representation does not make America's streets any safer. Indeed, when shoddy trial lawyering results in a false conviction, the real killer is left at large. It is a bad deal for juries, which have the right to all available evidence and mitigating circumstances in murder trials. Indeed, it is becoming increasingly common for jurors to recant their "guilty" votes when they learn, months or years later, of crucial evidence withheld by prosecutors or uninvestigated by the defense.

Many cases have gone to court a second, even third time—at vast expense to taxpayers—the result not of "coddling criminals" but of states refusing to pay for an adequate defense the first time around.

And more broadly, the sorry state of death-row lawyering undermines the protections the legal system affords all Americans and erodes the confidence of Americans in their courts. This is not a matter of liberal or conservative, Democrat or Republican. The fact is that for the indigent, "meticulous litigation" is a myth—indeed more of a myth than ever before. Every day, America is executing individuals for one crime only: the crime of being poor. Equal justice under law is nothing but an empty slogan when the resources so fundamental to its attainment are unavailable.

CHAPTER 4

A Question of

Innocence

"The execution of a person who can show that he is innocent comes perilously close to simple murder."
—JUSTICE HARRY BLACKMUN, 1992

Tall, deliberate of movement, his voice carefully modulated, Delbert Tibbs is a man of unusual gravity. A youth counselor at Hull House, the famous Chicago social-work agency founded by Jane Addams, Tibbs conveys a moral center that in even a brief conversation you know you could bet your life upon. Nothing in his demeanor conveys the essential fact that Delbert Tibbs was once a condemned man, or that his case was once so well known that almost 30 years ago his name adorned a mural on a Chicago railway overpass.

In 1974, Delbert Tibbs was arrested in Florida for a rape and murder he did not commit. At the time a theology student on a visit to Florida, he was not even in the same part of the state where the crime occurred. But he was an African-American, traveling alone, and the victim was white. Tibbs was convicted and sentenced to die in Florida's electric chair. Tibbs spent seven years fighting execution before he was fully vindicated when the original prosecutor admitted Tibbs's case had been tainted from the beginning.

In November of 1998, Delbert Tibbs joined 28 other individuals who had been similarly betrayed by the American judicial system. They assembled in Chicago for the first-ever conference on false conviction and the death penalty. Like Delbert Tibbs those 28 had all been falsely accused, falsely convicted, sentenced to die, and exonerated only after years of imprisonment; some came within hours of execution.

Until recently, few Americans believed that factually innocent individuals could in any large numbers find themselves on death row. The idea of executing an innocent prisoner is so shocking and repugnant to most of us that it is hard to comprehend its reality. It is easier to think—as hard-line death-penalty advocates still claim—that even when convictions are overturned, it is happening on "technicalities."

Yet the evidence is overwhelming and was only partially represented at that Chicago conclave. At this writing, 86 factually innocent individuals have been released from death rows around the country since the U.S. Supreme Court allowed executions to resume in 1976. This amounts to one complete exoneration for every eight executions, a staggering indicator of the unreliability of the criminal justice process. In fact, the number is likely higher. Scholars Hugo Adam Bedau of Tufts University and Michael Radelet of Florida State University have spent the past 30 years identifying more than 400 cases in which the defendant was wrongly convicted of a crime punishable by death.

Incredibly, some politicians claim that the existence of these 100 near martyrs proves, in the words of former Illinois governor Jim Edgar, that "the system works." Yet it was not the judicial system that freed the Ford Heights Four, young men falsely convicted of two brutal 1981 murders in a Chicago suburb. They walked out of Illinois prisons in 1996—two from death row, two from life terms—because Northwestern University journalism professor David Protess and his investigative reporting students decided to make the cases a class project—as a later Protess class did for Anthony Porter. It was not "the system" that freed Walter McMillan in Birmingham, Alabama, convicted of murder on the word of jailhouse informants. It was the accidental discovery of a tape that proved the snitches had fabricated their account. A lucky break on the way to the grave. The 86 innocence cases dating back to the 1970s are replete with such chance salvation: the evidence hidden in a prosecutor's desk drawer, the crucial witness arrested as a con man, the real murderer caught in a similar offense.

The existence of so many exonerated death-row inmates raises another and even more disturbing question: Has anyone in the United States been executed for a crime he or she did not commit? The dead tell no tales, so proving innocence after execution is fraught with ambiguity. But the evidence is unsettling. Bedau and Radalet report 28 executions of demonstrably innocent individuals prior to 1973. In 2000, researchers at the Quixote Center of Maryland identified no fewer than 16 individuals who since 1976 "were executed despite compelling evidence of their innocence." Investigative reporters at the *Chicago Tribune* uncovered four cases of executed inmates in which innocence appeared a strong probability.

Just how solid is the evidence of these false executions? Consider the case of Brian Baldwin, charged with the 1977 murder of

16-year-old Naomi Rolon in Alabama. Baldwin, at the time, was 17 and had escaped from a North Carolina youth detention center with a fellow juvenile offender named Edmund Horsley. Both of these teenagers were African-Americans. The two hitched a ride with Rolon, who was white, in North Carolina. The three drove into Alabama. There, Horsley drove off with Rolon and Brian Baldwin continued on his own. When Rolon's body was found beaten to death, both teens were arrested for her murder. Horsley named Baldwin, Baldwin signed a confession, and the two were convicted in separate trials.

Baldwin's trial—lasting one and a half days, including jury selection, hearing, deliberation, and sentencing—was like a catalogue of what can go wrong in a death-penalty case. Prosecutors deliberately excluded all African-American persons from the jury, a practice deemed unconstitutional by the U.S. Supreme Court a few years later. Indeed, an Alabama court later found that the prosecutor and judge in the case had for years practiced "deliberate racial discrimination." Baldwin's defense lawyer met with the young man for a total of 20 minutes before the trial, never conducted an investigation, presented no witnesses, and did not prepare Baldwin for testifying.

In retrospect, the trial was less notable for what happened in court than for what Baldwin's jury did not learn. The jury never learned that police had repeatedly beaten Baldwin and tortured him with a cattle prod until he confessed. The jury never learned that Baldwin's "confession" named the wrong weapon and the wrong method for Rolon's killing. The jury never learned that Horsley's statement, pointing to Baldwin as the killer, did describe her killing accurately. The jury never learned that forensics showed Naomi Rolon's killing to be the work of a left-handed assailant—and Horsley, not Baldwin, was left-handed. The jury never learned that Horsley's clothes were stained with blood and Baldwin's clothing tested negative for any blood at all. Baldwin was sentenced to die in Alabama's electric chair.

If all of this sounds like the basis for "reasonable doubt," such doubt was never reflected by appeals courts. The first appeal in the case was assigned to Baldwin's original trial judge—who, not surprisingly, upheld his own decision. When his postconviction lawyers uncovered the tainted confession and forensic evidence, the Alabama Court of Criminal Appeals denied Baldwin a chance to present this suppressed evidence in a hearing—provoking 33 prosecutors and judges across the country into filing a brief on Baldwin's behalf. Baldwin's co-defendant, Edmund Horsley, eventually confessed in a letter that he alone killed Naomi Rolon and that Baldwin knew nothing about the killing until his arrest. Yet the U.S. Court of Appeals for the Eleventh Circuit and the U.S. Supreme Court both refused to permit Baldwin an opportunity to present any new evidence. Baldwin was strapped into Alabama's electric chair on June 18, 1999, and executed after an hour's wait while technicians adjusted the machinery.

Brian Baldwin's execution shocks the conscience. But examined dispassionately, it is also a road map to the land of false conviction, a land ruled by police misconduct, suppressed evidence, botched forensics, and false confessions. The same year Baldwin was executed, Professor James Liebman of Columbia University released a landmark study reviewing every capital murder case between 1973 and 1995. Liebman revealed what he called "a broken system" of death-penalty trials. According to Liebman's analysis, state and federal courts found "grave constitutional error" in two-thirds of the capital cases they reviewed—not technicalities but fundamental miscarriages of justice. In 19 percent of those cases— one out of five—police or prosecutors actively suppressed evidence of innocence. Another 19 percent of cases were tainted by coerced confessions, jailhouse informants of dubious reliability, the systematic exclusion of black jurors, and other abuses. The Quixote Center's analysis of 16 possibly false executions like Baldwin's found the same factors, along with rampant incompetence at trial by death-penalty defense lawyers.

Broken down in academic studies, these false convictions appear as cool and manageable if disturbing statistics. But the reality is about the emotional vulnerability of individuals when confronted with the power and resources of police and prosecutors.

Consider the cases of Christopher Ochoa and Richard Danziger. In 1988, a 20-year-old woman named Nancy DePriest was raped and shot to death in a North Austin Pizza Hut where she worked. Police arrested and questioned Ochoa, barely out of his teens, threatening him with the death penalty if he did not confess. Finally Ochoa broke, admitted to the crime, and implicated his 19-year-old friend Danziger. Ochoa's confession was riddled with inaccurate descriptions of the crime, which police changed in their reports. Neither man ended up on death row, but given the crime that was a matter of chance rather than legal balance. Both Ochoa and Danziger received life sentences, and once in prison, Danziger was beaten so badly that he was left permanently disabled.

In 1996—eight years later—another inmate, Achim Josef Marino, wrote Governor George W. Bush confessing to Nancy DePriest's murder. "You all are legally and morally obligated to contact Danziger and Ochoa's attorneys and families concerning this confession," he wrote, adding a host of details that could only be known by the real killer. But the letter was buried in the governor's files. It was not until 2000, when Ochoa and Danziger had been incarcerated for 12 years and Governor Bush was on the presidential campaign trail, that the University of Wisconsin Innocence

Project arranged DNA testing—testing that fully exonerated both men and confirmed Marino's confession.

If false confession is a reality, so is an equally disturbing phenomenon: false science. Police crime labs, designed to provide objective evidence, too often turn into nothing more than tools of prosecution. In at least three states—West Virginia, Texas, and Oklahoma—hundreds of convictions have been reopened after crime-lab scientists were accused of doctoring or bungling forensic test results. In Oklahoma alone, 23 inmates were sent to death row between 1980 and 2001 based upon forensic evidence developed by Oklahoma City police laboratory scientist Joyce Gilchrist. By early 2001 ten of those men had been executed when an FBI review exonerated a rape suspect imprisoned for 16 years on the basis of Gilchrist's forensic testimony. The FBI found that Gilchrist, as *The New York Times* reported, "had misidentified evidence or given improper courtroom testimony in at least five of eight cases" reviewed by the feds. Over the years Gilchrist had been censured by judges, expelled from a forensic scientists' professional organization, and criticized by colleagues—yet continued to send defendants to prison and to death row. Gilchrist is not alone. The former head of West Virginia's crime lab, Fred Zain, was indicted for fraud in 1999 after the West Virginia Supreme Court found he had offered false testimony in hundreds of cases.

Professor Samuel Gross of the University of Michigan Law School believes that in death-penalty cases, false convictions are even more likely than in other criminal cases—thanks to the public pressure to solve heinous crimes, the power of prosecutors to select execution-friendly juries, and the special demands on defense attorneys, who must prepare not only for trial but for sentencing hearings.

The abuses so evident in Brian Baldwin's execution and in those academic studies can be unpacked in minute particulars in the cases of individuals freed from death row. For official misconduct, for instance, it is hard to beat the case of James Richardson of Florida. Richardson was convicted of poisoning his own children and sentenced to death in 1968. The threat of execution was removed when the Supreme Court overturned all existing death sentences in 1972. Seventeen years later, Janet Reno, then Dade County State's Attorney, was appointed special investigator in Richardson's case and concluded that the state had "knowingly used perjured testimony and suppressed evidence helpful to the defense." Richardson was freed 21 years after being sentenced to death and long after he would have been executed had not the Supreme Court enacted its brief national moratorium on execution.

Michael Mello, the veteran death-row appeals lawyer, finds the genesis of wrongful death-penalty convictions in deeply rooted social prejudices. For years, he defended death-row inmates in Florida, a state with the dubious distinction of more death-row exonerations than any other. His final case involved a motorcycle-gang member named Joe Spaziano convicted of murder solely on the basis of a single eyewitness. Spaziano's jury never learned that his accuser, a teenage boy, was a habitual user of LSD, and that his accusation—which he later recanted—emerged only under hypnosis carried out by a charlatan who had already been responsible for the near execution of two African-Americans in one of Florida's most famous death-row exonerations.

Mello sees a pattern in death-row innocence cases that is equal parts corruption and simple human failings. "Most of the accused individuals," Mello writes, "were in some sense 'others,' members of discrete and insular minorities marginalized and despised by

Florida's dominant culture (white, male, affluent)." Some, he says, were African-American; some, including his client Spaziano, were bikers or members of other socially marginal subcultures. In each case, he says, "cops or prosecutors or both succeeded in hiding from defense lawyers important evidence suggesting their innocence."

Indeed, says Mello, the "technicalities" that many of us assume are used to free the guilty are in fact systematically used to railroad the innocent.

> When their postconviction lawyers and investigators were finally able to unearth that evidence of innocence (and more, much more), the prosecutors deployed an arsenal of legal technicalities to persuade the courts not even to consider the newly discovered evidence of total factual innocence (by asserting that the innocents had found new evidence too late, or they'd filed in the wrong court at the wrong time, or whatever). In every case the state denied, loudly and publicly, that the defendant was innocent at all, even in the face of overwhelming evidence to the contrary.

It is the U.S. Supreme Court that has raised the practice of execution-by-technicality to an art form. In 1992 the Court heard the case of Lionel Herrera of Texas, who had affidavits and polygraph evidence from eyewitnesses denying his involvement in the murder for which he had been convicted. Among the new evidence was an affidavit from an attorney and former Texas judge who represented Lionel Herrera's brother Raul, who had since died. He said that Raul had confessed to the crime for which Lionel Herrera was now condemned.

By a 6–3 majority, the Supreme Court ruled that federal courts had little license to intervene in a case like Herrera's, to consider evidence of innocence unavailable at trial. Effectively, Chief Justice Rehnquist writing for the Court majority washed the judiciary's hands of responsibility for all but the most extreme innocence cases: "History shows that the traditional remedy for claims of innocence based on new evidence . . . has been executive clemency." Rehnquist warned of "the disruptive effect that entertaining claims of actual innocence would have on finality in capital cases, and the enormous burden that having to retry cases based upon stale evidence would place upon the States." In a concurring opinion, Justice Antonin Scalia—joined by Justice Clarence Thomas—went even further: "There is no basis in text, tradition, or even contemporary practice . . . for finding in the Constitution a right to demand judicial consideration of newly discovered evidence brought forward after conviction." Justice Harry Blackmun, writing for the Court's three dissenters, found such logic "perverse," and declared it "indecent" for federal courts to ignore evidence of innocence. Lionel Herrera was executed a few months later.

The Supreme Court's finding in Herrera is so stunning that it is worth repeating: evidence of innocence is no bar to execution. As the final date comes closer in capital cases, the legal system becomes locked in a battle over procedural issues rather than in a search for the truth.

The Supreme Court is not alone in its apparent tolerance for the execution of an occasional innocent individual. Several years ago, after an Illinois legislator first proposed the moratorium on executions that was ultimately enacted by Governor George Ryan in January 2000, the response of Illinois State Senator James "Pate" Philip reveals just how little it matters in today's propunishment climate whether the system works or not. Philip was reminded that

Illinois has exonerated nine death-row inmates over the last several years. Philip: "In what, 150 years, 175 years, that's less than one a year." Or as Dudley Sharp of the pro-execution Texas group Justice for All puts it, "When we use vaccines, we accept that a certain number of people are going to get sick and die from their use." It's considered politically palatable, in other words, to suggest a tolerable level of false execution.

Even as death-row exonerations rise in visibility and number—the Death Penalty Information Center reports that an average of 4.8 individuals are now freed from death rows every year—the possibilities for vindication have grown more and more restricted as legislators tag capital punishment to more and more offenses. Many of the 100 exonerated individuals started fighting for their lives before Congress defunded the nation's death-row resource centers, which provided appellate lawyers and investigative resources. Most secured their release before Congress in 1996 gutted habeas corpus—the long-venerated right of state prisoners to seek hearings in federal court—with the Antiterrorism and Effective Death Penalty Act.

This recent rush to execution is a terrifying development in American law. It reflects not a sound route to safe streets, but political cynicism and arrogance by legislators and judges who shred constitutional protections. After years of defending death-row clients—including the most guilty and vicious, such as serial killer Ted Bundy, as well as the most innocent—Mello is convinced that it is "the state's lack of humility in the face of an irrevocable penalty . . . that ought to give capital punishment proponents pause."

This is why simple reforms to the capital-trial apparatus are not enough. The bottom-line issue is human fallibility. Put in all the procedural protections in the world—spend millions on capital-trial defense and appeals—and you will eliminate many errors, perhaps save some innocent lives. But you will not eliminate false conviction. Supreme Court Justice Thurgood Marshall once said, "No matter how careful courts are, the possibility of perjured testimony, mistaken honest testimony, and human error remain all too real. We have no way of judging how many innocent persons have been executed, but we can be certain that there were some." We will always have mistakes, human error, and perjury. We will always have a rush to justice, hysterical public opinion, and political pressure. As long as we have these problems, innocent people will be convicted and sent to jail. And as long as we have the death penalty, innocent people will die, with no chance of correcting the error.

CHAPTER 5

Deadly Numbers: Race and the

Geography of Execution

"Having a white victim increases the probability of a death sentence by a greater amount than smoking increases the probability of heart disease."
—PROFESSOR MICHAEL RADALET

"Since you're the nigger, you're elected."
—POLICE OFFICER TO CLARENCE BRANDLEY, 1980

In February of 1978, Warren McCleskey and three other men robbed a furniture store in Fulton County, Georgia. Their break-in set off a silent alarm. Officer Frank Schiatt responded to the scene; McCleskey shot and killed him. Of that there was no question.

Sometimes, though, guilt can be just as revealing of injustice as innocence. When in 1987 the Supreme Court took up McCleskey's appeal while he languished on Georgia's death row, the question was not whether McCleskey had killed, but what was motivating

Georgia to kill McCleskey. For if there was no question about Warren McCleskey's guilt, there was also no doubt about three other
essential facts. First, McCleskey was black. Second, his victim, Officer Schiatt, was white. And third, in Georgia the killers of white victims were four times more likely to be sent to death row than the
killers of blacks. Was McCleskey facing execution for the crime he
had committed—or for the colors of his and his victim's skin? It's a
crucial question that—as the Supreme Court recognized in taking
McCleskey's case—goes to the heart of the death-penalty debate.

One person who might have illuminated the question, had he
been invited to speak to the Supreme Court, was a former school
custodian named Clarence Brandley. But in 1987 Brandley was in
no position to put in an appearance in Washington; he resided on
Texas' death row. Like McCleskey, Brandley was black and had
been accused of murdering a white victim. Unlike McCleskey,
Brandley happened to be innocent.

The victim's name was Cheryl Dee Ferguson, a vibrant 16-year-
old who in 1980 was about to begin her junior year at Conroe High
School in Bellville, Texas. She was one of the most popular girls at
school, manager of the volleyball squad, 5'7" tall, with long blond
hair, hazel eyes, and an attractive smile. On Saturday morning, August 23, 1980, she disappeared from a volleyball practice after a
trip to the washroom. Two hours later, two janitors found Cheryl's
naked body in a dusty loft above the school's auditorium. The janitors were Henry "Icky" Peace and his supervisor, Clarence Brandley. Police immediately decided the two were prime suspects. They
were questioned, fingerprinted, and asked for hair and blood
samples. They both cooperated fully. In order to demonstrate his
innocence, Brandley, then 28, voluntarily gave the police samples

of his hair and clothing and submitted to a lie detector test, which he passed. But then a frightening thing happened. The police officer interviewing the two janitors told them, "One of the two of you is going to hang for this." Turning to Brandley, the officer added the unforgettable words at the top of this chapter: "Since you're the nigger, you're elected."

Texas Ranger Wesley Styles abandoned his vacation to lead the investigation. By the time he arrived in Conroe it was already August 29, nearly a week after Cheryl Dee Ferguson's murder. Conroe was in a state of shock. Parents threatened to keep their daughters home from school until the murderer was caught. Because school was scheduled to start the following Monday, Styles needed immediate results. Only a few hours after he took over the investigation, Styles arrested Brandley for Ferguson's killing.

From the very beginning, Brandley firmly insisted that he was innocent. The prosecution's case was based solely on weak circumstantial evidence, with no blood, DNA, hair, or fingerprint evidence. Even so, Brandley's trial ended in a hung jury: eleven to one in favor of conviction. The one dissenting member of the all-white jury was William Srack. Srack says that the other jurors called him "nigger-lover" during deliberations, and after the trial Srack was harassed with telephone calls threatening to get him for saving the "nigger."

The prosecution tried again. At the second trial, in February 1982, again before an all-white jury, Brandley was convicted of murder. The prosecutor had again used his peremptory strikes to eliminate all blacks from the jury pool. On Valentine's Day—the day after the jury announced its verdict—Judge Martin followed the jury's recommendation and sentenced Brandley to death.

Eleven months after the conviction, while Brandley's attorneys were preparing an appeal, they learned that 166 of the 309 exhibits used at trial, many of which offered grounds for appeal, had vanished. Among the missing exhibits was a sperm sample from the victim that could have proved Brandley's innocence with newly developed DNA testing methods. Also missing were hair samples found near the victim's vagina and on her socks. Three of these hairs were reddish blond, matching neither Brandley's nor Ferguson's. These too could have pointed to the real assailant.

Despite such irregularities, in May 1985, three years after Brandley's conviction, the Texas Court of Criminal Appeals affirmed the conviction and death sentence. A few months later Brandley was given his execution date: January 16, 1986.

In late 1985, Brandley's attorneys finally won a stay, because the state had lost or destroyed crucial evidence that could have led to a dismissal of the charges. At that same time, Brandley got his first real break: Brenda Medina, a woman from nearby Cut 'n' Shoot, Texas, came forward with possible evidence of Brandley's innocence. A former boyfriend, James Dexter Robinson, had confessed to her that he had raped and murdered a young girl about the time that Cheryl Ferguson was victimized. Robinson had been a janitor at Conroe High but had been fired about a month before the incident. After the rape-murder, Robinson fled to South Carolina, he told her, because he had "killed a girl" and had hidden the body.

When Medina learned that Brandley had been convicted of Ferguson's murder, she met with an attorney who directed her to tell her story to the district attorney. However, the district attorney did not believe Medina's story, and he did not tell Brandley's attorney about it. Instead, the story leaked out from the first attorney that Medina had consulted. In 1987, after six years of fruitless appeals and massive civil rights demonstrations in support of Brandley, the Texas Court of Criminal Appeals ordered an evidentiary hearing to investigate all the allegations that had come to light. Judge Perry Pickett wrote a stinging condemnation of the procedures the prosecution had used in Brandley's case, stating, "The court unequivocally concludes that the color of Clarence Brandley's skin was a substantial factor which pervaded all aspects of the State's capital prosecution of him."

Despite this finding, in late February 1987, Brandley was given a new execution date—March 26, 1987—barely a month away. A thousand citizens marched through the streets of Conroe protesting the scheduled execution. Amnesty International joined the protest and demanded a meeting with the governor. Brandley wrote his last will and testament, neatly packed his books and his belongings, and moved to the execution cell to begin his final good-byes. At the last minute, Texas' attorney general joined the cry for a delay of the execution order to allow Brandley's attorneys time to gather newly discovered evidence. A delay was granted, providing Brandley with precious breathing room.

In 1989, after a flurry of publicity that included a *60 Minutes* segment and a report on the *700 Club,* the Texas Court of Criminal Appeals reversed Brandley's conviction by a vote of six to three. Relying on the 1987 evidentiary hearing in which Judge Pickett found that the prosecutors had railroaded Brandley out of racially based motives, the appellate court ordered a new trial where Brandley would be allowed to present new evidence of his innocence. But he did not have to go through it one more time, for prosecutors decided to drop the charges because they felt they would lose a third trial.

Finally, in 1990, after spending nearly a decade on death row, Brandley was freed. He was then 38.

_____

Clarence Brandley landed on death row not just through a miscarriage of justice but through the particular racial topography of capital punishment, the very subject of the case of Warren Mc-Cleskey, which the Supreme Court was considering just as turmoil was breaking out over the Brandley case.

Most Americans who support capital punishment believe that the death penalty goes to those who are in some objective sense the worst offenders, guilty of the most evil acts: a serial killer like Ted Bundy, who was killed by the state of Florida in 1989; or Timothy McVeigh, the Oklahoma City bomber, whose execution was being prepared by the federal government as this book was written. Who is sentenced to life in prison and who receives the ultimate punishment is supposed to follow from objective factors within clear measure of jury, judge, and public: factors such as the violence and cruelty with which the crime was committed, a defendant's culpability or history of violence, and the number of victims involved.

The reality of death row is different. The reality of death row is far more often Clarence Brandley than Timothy McVeigh. The reality is that the death penalty is essentially an arbitrary punishment, a product not of blind justice but of geography and of ethnicity.

Start with geography. It probably comes as no surprise to learn that murders committed in certain regions of our country are much more likely to result in the death penalty than are murders in other regions. The southern states (Alabama, Arkansas, Florida, Georgia, Louisiana, Mississippi, North Carolina, Oklahoma, South Carolina, Texas, Virginia), home to roughly 26 percent of our nation's population, carried out 83 percent of our nation's executions between 1976 and 1995. If you commit murder in a southern state, you are roughly three times more likely to be executed for the crime there as elsewhere. And Texas—which accounts for little more than 6 percent of the nation's population—executed 245 death-row inmates between 1977 and early 2001, more than one-third of the national total of 706.

It may be more of a surprise to learn that even the *federal* death penalty is just as subject to the whims of geography. According to the U.S. Department of Justice, 80 percent of all the federal death-penalty charges brought by prosecutors come from just five of the country's 92 judicial districts.

Another crucial geographically driven variable is mental impairment. Thirteen states forbid the execution of the mentally retarded; as a result, Rickie Ray Rector or Wanda Jean Allen, each with an IQ barely above 50, faced execution in Arkansas and Oklahoma but would have been spared in Georgia, the first state to rebel against this indefensible practice. (Executing the mentally impaired, which the Supreme Court was reconsidering as this book was written, is not just inhumane. It also raises the most profound questions of due process, given the limited ability of the mentally retarded to properly assist in their own defense. Human Rights Watch has noted in a report that "Offenders with mental retardation are particularly vulnerable to the well-documented arbitrariness and high risk of error in U.S. capital trials.")

And geography can determine who lives and who dies even within a single small state. Five of Connecticut's seven death-row inmates as of March 2001, for instance, were prosecuted in a single county, thanks to the zeal of a single state's attorney. By prosecutorial whim, a defendant in the city of Waterbury is far more likely to face lethal injection than a killer in the city of New Haven, just 40 miles away. In Pennsylvania, Philadelphia District Attorney Lynne Abraham seeks the death penalty in 85 percent of murder cases, 11 times more frequently than her counterpart in Pittsburgh.

Philadelphia alone is responsible for half of Pennsylvania's 223 death-row inmates—even though the city holds just 14 percent of the state's population.

What about race? The relationship between race and capital punishment is in fact complex. It is a fact, for instance, that more white defendants than black defendants have been executed. Between 1976 and 1995, according to the Death Penalty Information Center, 56 percent of the condemned prisoners executed were white, 38 percent black, and 6 percent Hispanic, Native American, or Asian. And death-row population statistics reflect similar percentages. As of January 1996, 48 percent of the inmates on death row were white, 41 percent were black, 7.5 percent were Hispanic, and 3.5 percent were listed as "other."

Yet there is a special relationship between the death penalty and African-Americans, a relationship going back to antebellum days, when the gallows was a principle means of punishing slaves, and on through the worst years of Jim Crow. Of 455 executions for rape in the United States between 1935 and 1967, 398—87 percent—were of African-Americans. Today, African-American defendants like Clarence Brandley are far more likely to receive the death penalty than are white defendants charged with the same crime. And black defendants, along with Latinos, are sentenced to death far out of proportion to their presence in the population.

For instance, African-Americans make up 25 percent of Alabama's population, yet 43 percent of Alabama's death-row inmates and 71 percent of those actually executed since 1976 are black. The population of Georgia's Middle Judicial Circuit is 40 percent black, but 77 percent of the circuit's capital decisions as of 1996 had been found against black defendants. The same state's Ocmulgee Judicial Circuit posts remarkably similar numbers. In 79 percent of the cases in which the district attorney sought the death penalty the defendant was black, despite the fact that only 44 percent of the circuit's population is black.

It is tempting to see such figures as a regional problem for the South. They aren't. The country as a whole does no better, and never has. The long legacy of slavery—the devaluing of African-American lives—has marked the federal death penalty from the moment the Constitution was drafted. Between 1789 and 1967, the federal government executed 336 men and four women. Of those, a staggering 61 percent were minorities: black (35 percent), Native American (19 percent), and Hispanic (7 percent). If you count only the federal executions since 1900, precisely the same margin holds: 61 percent of all federal killings this century were members of minority groups.

And what about our own time? Early in 2000, with the first federal executions since 1976 approaching, Attorney General Janet Reno commissioned a detailed study of all pending federal capital cases. The resulting report—"The Federal Death Penalty: A Statistical Survey," published in September 2000—left Reno, a death-penalty supporter, deeply shaken. Among its findings:

- 80 percent of all federal death-penalty charges referred by prosecutors for the attorney general's approval are African-American or Hispanic;
- 72 percent of active death-penalty cases approved by the attorney general have been members of minorities;
- White defendants are twice as likely as blacks and Hispanics to escape capital charges through plea agreements.

If the race of the defendant alters the death-penalty calculus, the race of the victim—more specifically, whether or not the victim was white—can have an even stronger influence. That same Justice Department study, for instance, revealed that U.S. attorneys are twice as likely to seek the death penalty for African-American defendants when the victim is not black.

The definitive evidence of the role played by a victim's skin color was compiled in the 1970s and 1980s by Professor David Baldus of the University of Iowa. Baldus's scholarship—taking apart more than 2,500 Georgia murder cases—formed the backbone of Warren McCleskey's appeal to the Supreme Court.

Controlling for 230 nonracial factors in the cases, Baldus found that defendants accused of murdering a white victim are 4.3 times more likely to receive the death penalty than defendants accused of killing blacks. Baldus determined that the race of the murderer was less important than the race of the victim. Fewer than 40 percent of the homicide victims in Georgia are white, yet fully 87 percent of the cases resulting in the death penalty involved white victims.

Baldus cited one judicial circuit in Georgia where 85 percent of the cases in which the district attorney sought the death penalty were against murderers of whites—even though 65 percent of the county's murder victims were African-Americans. Overall, this particular district attorney sought the death penalty in 34 percent of the cases involving white victims but a mere 5.8 percent of the cases in which the victim was black.

Georgia is not the only state where the color of the victim's skin can mean the difference between life and death. Nationwide, even though 50 percent of murder victims are African-American, says the Death Penalty Information Center, almost 85 percent of the victims in death-penalty cases are white. And in their 1989 book, *Death and Discrimination: Racial Disparities in Capital Sentencing,* Samuel Gross and Robert Mauro analyzed sentencing in capital cases in Arkansas, Florida, Georgia, Illinois, Mississippi, North Carolina, Oklahoma, and Virginia during a period when these states accounted for 379 of the 1,011 death penalties nationwide. They found widespread discrepancies in sentencing based on the victim's race in all eight states.

Indeed, as one study after another confirmed the correlation between the race of the homicide victim and whether the defendant would receive a capital sentence, the evidence became so overwhelming that Congress's General Accounting Office decided to take up the question itself. In its February 1990 report "Death Penalty Sentencing," the GAO reviewed 28 studies based on 23 sets of data and concluded, "In eighty-two percent of the studies, race of the victim was found to influence the likelihood of being charged with capital murder or receiving the death penalty, i.e., those who murdered whites were found more likely to be sentenced to death than those who murdered blacks."

And when a case involves interracial murder, the bias against black homicide defendants multiplies the effects of the bias against the murderers of white victims. Astoundingly, African-Americans who murder whites are 19 times as likely to be executed as whites who kill blacks.

Race of the defendant, race of the victim. There is one final variable: *the race of the jury.* For decades, prosecutors in capital cases used their "peremptory strikes"—the right of either side to reject a number of prospective jurors—to keep African-Americans off capital cases with black defendants, making the all-white jury something of a tradition.

In 1968, the Supreme Court declared such overt racism grounds for a mistrial. But in 1985, the U.S. Supreme Court in a ruling written by Chief Justice William Rehnquist gave prosecutors another, more subtle avenue for leveraging racial bias into death sentences. In *Wainright* v. *Witt,* the Court gave prosecutors unprecedented power to reject any jurors who harbor doubts about capital punishment. With African-Americans and women, on average, more skeptical of capital punishment than white males, the results are devastating. One 1982 North Carolina jury study found 55.2 percent of black potential jurors being instantly excluded during the death-penalty qualifying process in contrast to 20.7 percent of whites.

South Carolina capital defense lawyer David Bruck has described death-qualification as "ethnic cleansing" of the jury pool: "Death-qualifying a jury basically eliminates half of the potential black jurors," he points out. Savvy prosecutors can then use their peremptory challenges to eliminate many of the African-American or female jurors who remain, without seeming to apply the broad brush of racism.

The impact of this "ethnic cleansing" on capital trials is immediate and specific. In the 1982 Philadelphia murder trial of Mumia Abu-Jamal, for instance, prosecutors first eliminated 20 black potential jurors through death-qualification—then struck another 11 African-Americans through peremptory challenges. The result, notes journalist David Lindorff, who has covered Abu-Jamal's case in depth: "In a city that is almost 44 percent black, the former Black Panther ended up with a single African-American on the jury that convicted him and sentenced him to death." Abu-Jamal's experience is far from unique. Capital juries are today nearly as racially imbalanced as they were when race alone was grounds for a peremptory strike.

Most of this evidence was already known by 1987, when lawyers from the NAACP Legal Defense and Education Fund brought

Warren McCleskey's appeal to the Supreme Court. McCleskey's attorneys laid the vast accumulated statistical data about the race of defendants, the race of victims, and the racial makeup of juries at the feet of the Supreme Court.

The Supreme Court's response has shaped the criminal justice system ever since. By a narrow 5–4 majority, the Supreme Court denied McCleskey's petition. The statistics are true, wrote Justice Lewis Powell for the majority, and indeed shows "a risk" that death sentences are related to race. And yet the data are still irrelevant. The only question was whether McCleskey could show "exceptionally clear proof" that an individual judge or jury or prosecutor acted "in *his* case with discriminatory purpose." Powell and the Court majority explicity refused to question the bias of the system as a whole, because, Justice Powell wrote, that would challenge "decisions at the heart of the state's criminal justice system," the discretion of prosecutors and judges. Georgia executed Warren McCleskey in its electric chair on September 25, 1991.

Only four years after the McCleskey decision, an interviewer asked newly retired Justice Powell if he regretted his vote in any case in his career. Yes, he replied: *McCleskey* v. *Kemp*. "I have come to think capital punishment should be abolished" because of the deeply embedded inequities in the justice system, Justice Powell said. By then, the McCleskey ruling had already accelerated a flood of racially clouded death sentences. By ten years after the McCleskey decision, 115 black men had been executed for killing white victims since the death penalty's restoration; only *seven* white men had been executed for murdering blacks. In response to the McCleskey decision, the Racial Justice Act was introduced in Congress in 1994. The purpose of the act was to allow condemned prisoners to appeal their death sentences using evidence of past discriminatory sentencing—the kind of evidence that failed to save McCleskey. After passing in the House 217–212, the bill failed in the Senate. It has never been revived.

"The death penalty," says Bryan Stevenson, director of the Equal Justice Initiative of Alabama, "symbolizes whom we fear and don't fear, whom we care about and whose lives are not valid." With black men nearly eight times more likely to be victims of homicide than white men, could there be a more blatant message from the criminal justice system that it values some lives more highly than others? Quietly and methodically, one prosecution at a time, our judicial system is telling us that African-American life is less important than white life, and its annihilation less tragic.

In *Furman* v. *Georgia* in 1972, the Supreme Court first asked whether an equitable application of capital punishment is ever possible in a nation where racism and discrimination are so thoroughly woven into the fabric of everyday life. Reaffirming the constitutionality of the death penalty four years later, the Court majority answered in the affirmative. The combined impact of Mc-Cleskey and other recent Supreme Court decisions has been to embed racism and economic bias ever more deeply in capital punishment. This self-evident inequity—now at the heart of America's capital trials—erodes, rather than enhances, public confidence in the justice system.

CHAPTER 6

False Closure: Victim Rights

Versus Vengeance Rights

The blue and white flames shot from Pedro Medina's head for 10 seconds. The smell of burned flesh caused witnesses to gag. But Florida's grisly 1997 execution of Medina for the murder of schoolteacher Dorothy James inspired little sympathy in official quarters. "My compassion is with the victim of the crimes. I really don't have that much compassion for people on death row," said the state's Democratic attorney general, Bob Butterworth; declared state house Republican leader Buzz Ritchie, "If anything, we ought to take a moment to reflect upon the pain and suffering of the victim."

In arguments over the death penalty, "the pain and suffering of the victim" is the trump card. The death penalty may not make society any safer, trials may not be fair, but justice for murder victims and their survivors requires that a life be taken. "I hear the tortured voices of the victims crying out to me for vindication," U.S. Court of Appeals judge Alex Kozinski writes. Judge Kozinski has sometimes considered appeals from those sentenced to die in the final hours before they will be strapped to a gurney or into an electric chair. He says he long ago concluded that capital punishment has no deterrent value and is riddled with discrimination against the poor and minority groups. Yet, he says, it is to honor victims that he still signs off on executions.

But which victims do Ritchie and Butterworth and Judge Kozinski have in mind? Whose vindication? Not Lindi James, the daughter of the woman Pedro Medina was convicted of killing. Though pointedly ignored by prosecutors and the press, she forcefully opposed the death sentence handed Medina, a Cuban immigrant with a lifetime of psychiatric hospitalizations. "This is almost impossible for me to talk about anymore," Lindi James said shortly after Medina's execution. "I am exhausted. I spent years trying to get people to listen." While Florida's politicians grandstanded about victim rights, Dorothy James was "vindicated" against her own family's wishes.

The belief that capital punishment vindicates the dead and provides surviving family members with closure is central to the debate over America's death penalty. On the eve of executions, televison cameras juxtapose anti-execution protesters with surviving family members. Self-described victim-rights groups run out of office any judges deemed "soft" on the death penalty. "Crime victims are the sleeping giant in this state," exulted one Tennessee district attorney in 1995 after victim advocates forced the ouster of Judge Penny J. White because of her vote against a single death sentence. Victim rights equals vengeance rights.

Yet a growing chorus of murder victims' families is, like Lindi James, rejecting the role of executioner and insisting that victim rights and vengeance rights are not the same. When two thugs in Laramie, Wyoming, hijacked Matthew Shepard, a gay college student, tied him to a fence, and beat him to death, prosecutors sought to execute his killers, Aaron McKinney and Russell Henderson. But Matthew's parents, Judy and Dennis Shepard, intervened to spare the killers' lives. "I would like nothing better than to see you die, Mr. McKinney," Dennis Shepard said in court. "However, this is the time to begin the healing process. To show mercy to someone who refused to show any mercy."

There are good reasons to take victim rights seriously. Anyone who has ever survived a violent crime or lost a family member to murder understands that the courts can easily revictimize victims. For too long the criminal-justice bureaucracy considered survivors of violence little more than convenient sources of evidence, offering them neither social services nor an independent voice in the proceedings. If the victims happened to be black or female or gay or Latino, their chances of being abused and disrespected by police or prosecutors or courts—their chances of being blamed for what happened to them—went from a possibility to near certainty.

Indeed, it was feminists who first challenged this victim-blaming in the 1970s with a successful national campaign to get respect and services for survivors of sexual assault.

But that welcome focus on victims was soon overrun by a far more partisan agenda: in the mid-1970s, conservative politicians hoping to ride the public's fear of crime into office co-opted the phrase "victim rights," converting it into code for restoring the death penalty and weakening protections for criminal defendants. Thus it was that in 1991 the Supreme Court permitted juries and judges to consider victim-impact testimony as one factor in death-penalty cases.

The Supreme Court has now permitted victim-impact testimony for nearly a decade. As it has turned out, some victims get decidedly more rights than others. Law professor Susan Bandes of

DePaul University in Chicago points out that using victim-impact testimony to help determine sentences in effect gives more articulate victims greater clout. What is more, in death-penalty cases, victims' voices are usually recognized by prosecutors and media only when they are on the side of killing. The Shepards were fortunate that a sympathetic prosecutor was persuaded by their calls for mercy. Far more often, surviving families who question the death penalty find themselves, like Lindi James, shamefully ignored.

Take the worst single act of mass murder in modern American history, the bombing of the Alfred P. Murrah Federal Building in Oklahoma City in 1995. When Timothy McVeigh stood trial in Denver—with little doubt as to his guilt—victims' wrenching testimony occupied center stage, as it should. Commentators extolled the role of victim-rights advocates in the case, the first large-scale demonstration of victims' new power in sentencing, and castigated the trial judge for suggesting that some of the emotion might be "inflammatory." "Closure" for Oklahoma City's victims became the watchword of television news anchors.

Amid this wave of victim consciousness, few seemed to notice that the whole process discriminated against survivors and relatives of victims who did not not favor the ultimate punishment for McVeigh. To put it more bluntly, any victim or relative who wanted to testify at McVeigh's sentencing first had to pass a death-penalty loyalty test.

One of those who didn't pass the loyalty test was Bud Welch, whose daughter Jennifer died in the Alfred P. Murrah building while he stood across the street. Welch supported capital punishment all his life, but after Jennifer's killing he changed his mind. "God only knows there's been enough bloodshed . . . we don't need any more death," he said. Instead of pushing for McVeigh's execution, Welch befriended McVeigh's father.

Surely Welch and other Oklahoma City victims who are opposed to execution deserved their own opportunity to seek "closure" by bearing witness in the legal record. But in Denver, as elsewhere in the federal court system, calling witnesses for victim-impact testimony is entirely up to the prosecution. In Denver, the prosecution didn't want Welch's qualms to interfere with a death sentence. He never testified.

Victims who do agree to testify often find themselves forbidden to air any doubts they may have about the death penalty. Just ask SueZann Bosler of Hallandale, Florida. Just before Christmas of 1986, Bosler's father, a minister in the Church of the Brethren, was stabbed 24 times by a 20-year-old burglar named James Campbell; Campbell also stabbed SueZann in the head, nearly fatally. Yet through three trials, SueZann Bosler protested the death sentence handed her father's killer. In the three separate trials, Bosler was required to recount the story of her father's murder and her own stabbing; each time, she was prohibited from telling a sentencing jury of her opposition to Campbell's execution, with the threat of being held in contempt of court if she spoke out. It took more than a decade for Bosler to at last persuade prosecutors to spare Campbell's life.

So much for victims' rights.

The emergence of anti-execution "survivors of homicide" like the Shepards, SueZann Bosler, and Bud Welch—in the face of hostility from prosecutors and the media—is in fact one of the most important developments on the criminal-justice scene. For one thing, those survivors challenge a vengeance-rights lobby that has sought a monopoly on the image of crime victims, an angry image exploited and perpetuated by politicians in ways that have nothing to do with victims' real interests or a balanced view of law and justice.

Often presenting itself as a grassroots victims' campaign, the vengeance-rights lobby has more to do with the prison-industrial complex than with victims' real needs. For instance, California's Doris Tate Crime Victims Bureau—the driving force behind the state's "three strikes" law and the state's expanded death penalty—gets 78 percent of its funding, along with free office space and lobbying staff, from the California Correctional Peace Officers Association, the prison guards' union, which has an obvious interest in longer, meaner sentences and a hard-line law-and-order climate.

But the importance of these victims goes far beyond politics. Anti-execution survivor-activists like Bud Welch challenge the popular proposition that crime victims can only be defined by their anger, that "closure" can only come through more killing. In fact, there is no evidence that executions provide surviving family members with the "closure" they are led to expect. Not a single psychological study of victims' families suggests any more healing or balance in the wake of an execution. "I have never met anyone who healed better because of an execution," says SueZann Bosler, who has spent much of the decade since her father's killing talking with dozens of victim-families. Execution, Bosler is convinced, represents nothing but "false closure."

It's natural, indeed inevitable, that extreme violence or loss provokes rage. But that rage is easily exploited and perpetuated by politicians in ways that have nothing to do with victims' real needs and interests, with untangling the Gordian knot of grief and anger and guilt that can beset any survivors of violence or their family members. Dr. Frank Ochberg, a psychiatrist, nationally prominent victim advocate, and a pioneering specialist in post-traumatic stress disorder, has written, "Survivors often do less hating than one might expect. . . . The co-victims, the next of kin of the injured and dead, are more often the ones moved to rage and vengeance, if not hatred." Ochberg is profoundly concerned about where such sentiments may lead: "Obsessive hatred," he writes, "is a corrosive condition." Corrosive and, ultimately, self-defeating.

If the death penalty does not serve any real need of surviving families—and since victims are so divided in their views—what "victim interests" are served? Not vindication, surely, just simple and brutal vengeance, with no other social or moral purpose. But the entire purpose of criminal law is to step between victimizer and victim, to substitute balanced justice for individual vengeance. Today's death penalty—and, in particular, the claim that it is somehow justified by victim rights—propels American law back to the era when family grievances were settled with shoot-outs, when unproven crimes were avenged by mobs at the end of a rope.

The great contribution of people like Dennis and Judy Shepard is to demonstrate that victim rights and vengeance rights are not synonymous—and that the victimized can rise above the violence of their victimizers. And there are alternatives for survivor-families. Instead of the false closure of the death penalty, a growing number of these survivor-families are piecing together their shattered lives by becoming full-time activists against the real roots of violence. Freddie Hamilton, a mother from Brooklyn, New York, lost her 14-year-old son, Njuzi Ray, to a street-corner shooting in 1993. Instead of demanding his killer's execution, she sued the gun makers who funneled all those weapons to Brooklyn in the first place—and won. In 1994 a paranoid schizophrenic gunman named Colin Ferguson opened fire on a Long Island Rail Road commuter train. Among Ferguson's victims were the husband and son of Carolyn McCarthy, a nurse from Mineola. Widowed, with her son paralyzed, McCarthy refused to argue for the death penalty for Ferguson. Instead, she, too, took on the gun lobby, and in 1996 won a seat in Congress against vehement opposition from the NRA. SueZann Bosler and Bud Welch both joined Murder Victims Families For Reconciliation, a national coalition against capital punishment.

The time is right to end the fiction that the death penalty serves the interests of victims. It is time to sever victim rights from vengeance rights once and for all. It is time to hear the voices of survivors like SueZann Bosler, who against all the force of the law and clichés of closure keeps insisting upon a simple point: "When the state kills somebody it is just making more victims—another mother without a son." When Judge Kozinski invokes "tortured voices of the victims crying out to me for vindication," the new generation of victim-activists reply: Not in my name.

CHAPTER 7

The Mark of Cain:

Faith and the Death Penalty

"When they're on the gurney, they're stretched out. I mean, his arms are extended. I've often compared it to a crucifixion kind of activity, only as opposed to the person upright, he is lying down."
—MICHAEL GRACZYK, ASSOCIATED PRESS REPORTER, HUNTSVILLE, TEXAS, WITNESS TO 170 EXECUTIONS

"If we were sitting in the high court, no man would ever have been executed."
—RABBI AKIBA AND RABBI TARFON, FIRST CENTURY

When in 1787 Dr. Benjamin Rush became the first American leader to propose abolishing the death penalty, he did not do so as a politician—though he was a politician, one of the signers of the Declaration of Independence. Instead, he took his position as a person of faith. "Laws which inflict death for murder," Dr. Rush wrote, "are, in my opinion, as unchristian as those which tolerate or justify revenge. . . . The power over human life is the sole prerogative of Him who gave it. Human laws, therefore, rise in rebellion against this prerogative, when they transfer it to human hands."

More than three centuries later, on Good Friday of 1999, America's Roman Catholic bishops called upon "all people of good will, and especially Catholics" to work actively against capital punishment. "Throughout the states," wrote the bishops, "more than 3,500 prisoners await their deaths. These numbers are deeply troubling. The pace of executions is numbing. The discovery of people on Death Row who are innocent is frightening."

What is the relationship between capital punishment and religious faith? In this country's intermingled religious heritage, capital punishment often seems to have history and tradition on its side. Jesus himself was the victim of capital punishment. The Mosaic Law upon which Christianity based its teachings lists 36 capital offenses, and for centuries the Christian churches that carried forward Jesus' message sanctioned brutal executions in large number.

Yet one of the most remarkable revolutions in American religious life has occurred in recent decades: the emergence of widespread opposition to capital punishment among leaders and laity of many of the country's largest and most influential denominations. Prior to 1950, only individual religious thinkers like Dr. Rush, along with a handful of small denominations or faith communities, like the Quakers and Dorothy Day's Catholic Worker movement, actively opposed capital punishment. Most religious leaders either outright endorsed the death penalty or remained silent.

What was it that changed in the last generation? Why is it that today, the bishops of the Roman Catholic Church, the councils of Conservative and Reform Judaisim, the Presbyterian Church, the United Methodist Church, the Lutheran Church, the Reformed Church, and the National Council of Churches are all on record against capital punishment? And why have some other Protestant denominations—most notably, the 16-million-strong Southern Baptists—resisted joining them?

Understanding what is emerging as a major confrontation between capital punishment and religious faith requires first contending with the relationship between religion and public life. When it comes to taking a public stand on an issue, vanity asks the question, "Is it popular?" Politics asks the question, "Is it expedient?" Religion asks the question, "Is it right?" At the core of every political, economic, or social issue are religious, moral, and spiritual dimensions. We are all spiritual, moral, social, economic, and political beings, whether or not we are aware of each dimension and how they interact. The ideal is to be conscious of and develop each and every dimension to its fullest capacity while maintaining a balance with the others. In religious tradition we are all equal before God, and should be equal before the law; our finitude—and for those in Christian tradition our sin—prevents us from achieving this ideal. Precisely because life is not an ideal, but real, we are constantly forced to make imperfect choices in an imperfect world.

When Jesus said, "Render therefore unto Caesar the things that are Caesar's; and unto God the things that are God's," he was saying and confirming that God is, government is, and each has its proper place. He was saying, I'll share with you some principles and the spirit with which to confront the world, but the circumstances of life are too intricate for me to give you a formula for every situation. Using your gifts of mind and spirit, and with God's help, do the best you can to answer the questions and deal with the issues as they arise. The constant struggle is to understand what is, and how the things that are Caesar's and the things that are God's interrelate and coexist with each other.

Politics does not create religious commitment; but for many, religion creates political commitment. The Bible's directive to feed the hungry may lead in a direct line from the hungry person; to one's own pantry; to the soup line; to the Agriculture Department; to national and international agriculture policies. Religious beliefs inform political beliefs.

Likewise, the issue of civil order leads from concern for those individuals who create civil disorder (criminals), and for their victims, to the means and issues involved in protecting civil order and maintaining a safe society (the judicial system, jails, and ultimately capital punishment).

One example of this volatile dynamic between religious faith and the debate over capital punishment came with the case of Karla Faye Tucker in Texas. Karla Faye Tucker was by her own account a child heroin addict and a teenage prostitute. In 1983 Tucker and her then-boyfriend murdered Jerry Lee Dean and Deborah Thornton, a woman Dean had taken home from an office party, with a pickax in retaliation for a dispute over a motorcycle. In prison, Karla Faye Tucker became an evangelical Christian. She married her prison pastor, Dana Brown. Tucker's case became widely known after she was interviewed on the *700 Club* and later on *Larry King Live.* The brother of Deborah Thornton joined the campaign to save Tucker's life (even though Thornton's husband fought for her execution). As Tucker exhausted her judicial appeals in late 1997, her cause was taken up by some of the country's most influential evangelicals, including Pat Robertson, who urged then-Governor George W. Bush to stay her execution and the Texas Board of Pardons and Paroles to commute her sentence.

After the U.S. Supreme Court turned down a final appeal, Governor Bush declined to stay Karla Faye Tucker's execution. At the time, he publicly said he "sought guidance from prayer," though later he privately ridiculed Karla Faye in an interview with conservative journalist Tucker Carlson, mimicking her appeals for mercy. When Karla Faye Tucker was strapped to the gurney on February 3, 1998, she apologized to the families of her victims and stated that she would soon be meeting Jesus; "I love you all very much" were her final words.

Karla Faye Tucker's execution distressed many conservative evangelical Christians who had been moved by her story. Through groups like Prison Fellowship Ministries, evangelical churches have in recent years begun involving themselves in greater numbers with prisoners. Tucker's execution caused widespread soul searching about the death penalty. The Rev. Richard Cizik, executive director of the National Association of Evangelicals representing some 42,000 churches, said Tucker's execution inspired "a certain moral revulsion" because "she was a person of such obvious spiritual change, a subject on which many Christian conservatives thought they had made up their minds." Pat Robertson denounced her execution. "There are times," Robertson said, "when justice must be trumped by mercy."

Some liberal commentators could not resist the temptation to be glib about such sentiments, remarking that the fact that Tucker was a white evangelical woman made her palatable to the media, which has rarely before looked a death-row inmate in the eye. But such comments miss the point. The fact was that millions of

Americans for the first time met a death-row inmate—an admitted ax murderer—in all her complication and contradiction. And nowhere was this challenge felt more acutely than among Christian conservatives, who compared Tucker's appeal for mercy with the imperatives of their faith. Instead of the constant drumbeat for vengeance, they heard a human being who like Christ on the cross could cry, "I thirst." (The Texas governor's callous joking about Karla Faye was reminiscent of the Roman soldiers who responded to Jesus' plea with a sponge soaked in vinegar.) As a result of that collision between the principles of faith and the specific particulars of an execution, the Rev. Robertson, the Rev. Richard Whitehead of the Rutherford Institute, and some other evangelical leaders have endorsed the call for a national moratorium on executions. Certainly not all Christian conservatives share their view. The Rev. Jerry Falwell, most prominently, has disputed Pat Robertson on the issue. But the fact remains that a sincere, deeply felt schism has opened in the ranks of religious conservatives over the death penalty—a schism that is likely to only deepen as the particulars of an escalating number of executions conflict with the very bedrock principles of Jesus' teaching.

Today's argument among Christian evangelicals about capital punishment mirrors decades of debates in other denominations. In one sense there is nothing new about such disputes: Many individual religious figures have debated capital punishment over the centuries. The Talmud, comprising centuries of Jewish commentaries on the Bible, records a debate about capital punishment among leading rabbis in the first century after the destruction of Jersualem. Jews, in the days of Rome, governed themselves with a high court called a Sanhedrin. One rabbi declares that it would be excessive and destructive for a Sanhedrin to order an execution once in seven years. Then a second rabbi says "once in 70 years." Then two of the most revered sages of Jewish history, Rabbi Akiba and Rabbi Tarfon, assert their complete opposition to capital punishment: "If we were sitting in the Sanhedrin, no man would ever have been executed." To which one final rabbi heatedly retorts— like Al Gore and George W. Bush insisting upon deterrence—that Akiba and Tarfon "would cause the proliferation of bloodshedders in Israel."

Christian thinkers, too, have sometimes spoken in conflicted voices about capital punishment. St. Augustine of Hippo, the most influential of early Christian writers, was of profoundly divided mind. In *The City of God,* Augustine defended the right of the state "to put criminals to death, according to law or the rule of rational justice." But in his letters, he took a different view, imploring fellow Christians to "not be provoked by the atrocity of . . . sinful deeds to gratify the passion for revenge." In one letter he pleads against the execution of the murderers of one priest and the mutilation of another. Do not let, he wrote, "the sufferings of the servants of God . . . be sullied with the blood of their enemies. . . . But, now that there is another possible punishment by which the mildness of the Church can be made evident, and the violent excess of savage men be restrained, why do you not commute your sentence to a more prudent and more lenient one?"

A succession of early Church leaders and secular rulers aligned with the Church would embrace Augustine's first view of the law as a sword of God, while ignoring his calls for mercy and his warning about the corrupting effects of execution. The Crusades solidified the idea of spreading Christianity at swordpoint. It was not until the twelfth century that a movement of Christian dissenters arose in France, founded by an itinerant street preacher named Waldès, which among other protests challenged Church doctrine on capital punishment. The Waldensians, as they were called, claimed that homicide of any sort was absolutely forbidden by the Fifth Commandment, and they argued that Christian laws, which should reflect Jesus' call for mercy and compassion, had grown more severe than the Mosaic laws they replaced. The Waldensians' challenge, writes James Megivern, a theologian and a leading historian of capital punishment, "had an impact that still reverberates. It seized the high moral ground and pointed out the worst features of the death penalty. . . . Such a radical critique of the very institution of capital punishment in a Christian context was unparalleled. It was an affront to the basic belief system of the period." The Waldensians were mercilessly suppressed by Church and state—so completely that today their arguments are known mainly from the words of their opponents. Ironically, the Church responded to the Waldensians by making ever more elaborate and prominent the theological defenses of the death penalty—theological defenses that by the fourteenth century formed the basis for massive bloodletting of supposed heretics during the Inquisition and that would shape many denominations' official thinking for centuries. By 1566, the Roman Catechism referred explicitly to state authority as "the legitimate avenger of crime," by death if necessary.

The Protestant Reformation, at first, offered little challenge to this reigning idea. "Let no one imagine that the world can be governed without the shedding of blood . . . for the world is wicked and bound to be so," Martin Luther wrote in 1524. In the early years of the Reformation, a few small Protestant sects challenged church-sanctioned killing of heretics in one way or another. But it was not until the late seventeenth century that the first concerted and sustained religious opposition to capital punishment took shape among England's Quakers, some 50 years ahead of Cesar Beccaria's treatise. Imprisoned as enemies of the Church of England, early Quakers saw up close the excesses of England's legal system, which had more than 150 capital laws on the books. The words of one early Quaker, George Fox, sound strikingly contemporary in an era in which three-strikes life terms are invoked for theft of a pizza and 15-year prison terms for minor drug offenses. Fox declared that laws that "struck down the thief who had filched only a small amount as well as the murderer, inevitably destroyed all sense of justice in the popular mind." Another Quaker thinker, John Bellers, went a step further, persuading fellow Quakers to campaign for "utter abolition of the death penalty" as an affront to the teachings of Jesus.

It was that Quaker religious tradition that dominated Pennsylvania in the eighteenth century and that shaped the thinking of Benjamin Rush, beginning America's long religious debate over capital punishment.

Yet it was only after World War II that larger American religious denominations took on the death penalty in an organized way. The executions of Julius and Ethel Rosenberg for espionage in 1953 was one trigger: some 2,300 clergy of various faiths had signed an appeal to President Eisenhower asking him to block the couple's killing. Pope Pius XII sought mercy for the Rosenbergs "out of motives of charity," an appeal the White House did not acknowledge.

New attention to capital punishment came with Caryl Chessman's best-selling death-row memoir, *Cell 2455 Death Row*, in 1955. By 1956, the Methodist Church became the first mainline Protestant denomination to go on record against the death penalty. In a resolution, the church stated, "We deplore the use of capital punishment." The United Methodist Church has reaffirmed the anti–death penalty statement every four years since. Within four years, the United Church of Canada, the American Baptists, the Union of American Hebrew Congregations, and the American Ethical Union had all joined with statements of moral opposition to capital punishment.

Debate was quietly mounting within the Roman Catholic Church as well—a debate accelerated by the reform-minded spirit of Pope John XXIII and Vatican II. A small but persistent group of Catholic clergy and lay leaders—most notably Father Donald Campion, a Jesuit priest, and Donal E. MacNamara, a lay Catholic leader and the dean of the New York Institute of Criminology— began calling for, in Campion's words, "a new emphasis on the notion of the inalienable rights of the human person."

Through the 1960s, a few other mainline church voices were added to the opposition, inspired in part by the civil rights movement's consciousness-raising around racial inequity in the criminal justice system. The United Church of Christ (1962), the Reformed Church (1965), the Presbyterian Church (1965–1966), and the Lutheran Church (1966) each passed resolutions opposing the death penalty. By 1968—a year after the last execution that would take place until 1977—the National Council of Churches was finally able to assemble enough votes from its member churches to go on record against capital punishment.

It was the debate over capital punishment in the Supreme Court in the 1970s that brought the next major step in the revolution in religious death-penalty activism. In 1972, the year the Supreme Court temporarily halted executions with *Furman* v. *Georgia,* the Roman Catholic bishops of Indiana broke with long-standing Church policy to call for abolition of the death penalty. In

1974, through its bishops, the Church issued a brief, but decisive, statement: "The U.S. Catholic Conference goes on record in opposition to capital punishment." Over the next decade, after the Supreme Court reinstated executions with *Gregg* v. *Georgia,* a growing number of Roman Catholic bishops protested the new wave of executions that commenced with Gary Gilmore in 1977. In part, this profound shift in the politics of American Catholicism reflected the rise of a younger generation of Church leaders shaped by the civil rights movement and the Vietnam War; and in part, it reflected recognition that the Catholic Church's "right-to-life" position on abortion was profoundly at odds with continued endorsement of capital punishment.

By 1980, the National Conference of Catholic Bishops debated and approved what has been described as "the most controversial vote ever taken" by that body: a full-length pastoral letter calling for the abolition of capital punishment. "It was one of the few documents I can remember which barely received the two-thirds majority of votes needed to pass," recalls the Most Rev. Peter Rosazza, Auxiliary Bishop of the Archdiocese of Hartford, Connecticut, who was part of that historic conclave.

By the early 1990s, American Catholic bishops were intervening with increasing visibility in America's death-penalty debate, citing what the late Cardinal Joseph Bernardin of Chicago called a "seamless garment" commitment to life. In 1995, Pope John Paul II ratcheted up the Church's opposition to capital punishment with the papal encyclical *Evangelium Vitae* (Gospel of Life). In what amounts to a revolutionary departure from centuries of Church teaching, Pope John Paul II states that the death penalty can only be justified to protect society from the actions of a dangerous individual—and this is ruled out by the security of modern prisons. Prison, says the Pope, renders capital punishment moot; there is always a better alternative. In 1998 John Paul II made it clear that this encyclical was no abstract rendering of philosophy when on a pastoral visit to St. Louis he asked Governor Mel Carnahan to commute the sentence of a condemned killer whose execution date was approaching—a step Governor Carnahan agreed to take.

All of this activity across denominational lines radically changed the terrain of the religious politics of the death penalty. And more conservative churches fought back. The National Association of Evangelicals (1972), the Lutheran Church's Missouri Synod (1976), and the National Association of Free Will Baptists (1977) all passed resolutions favoring capital punishment, while the Southern Baptist Convention has remained silent.

The advent of the death-penalty moratorium campaign promises to open a new chapter in religious activism against capital punishment. Religious organizations such as the Equal Justice USA Project of the Catholic-affiliated Quixote Center are at the heart of moratorium efforts. At the same time, however, too few of the denominations whose leadership bodies are on record against the death penalty have become involved at the level of congregation or parish. The next step is for clergy and congregations at the grassroots level to adopt a death-penalty moratorium as an issue— and, just as important, to let local prosecutors and judges know of their concern as a growing number of capital cases flood the courts. It remains a large challenge to convince church members and the general public of the moral, social, and economic bankruptcy of continuing to pursue a death-penalty policy.

And what, finally, about the Bible? Both religionists who support and religionists who oppose capital punishment try to show that the Bible supports them. In theological circles this is known as "proof-texting": finding a biblical text that "proves" your point, rather than explaining the text in context, then applying that central truth to a current situation.

Without being absolutist, it can be fairly stated that religious conservatives, who often read the Bible in more literal terms, use various scriptures to support their position in favor of capital punishment. Religious liberals, on the other hand, who tend to see the Bible in less literal terms, try to divine in scripture general principles and a spirit that combines the demands of justice tempered with mercy and grace. Religious liberals, more than religious conservatives, tend to accept and utilize modern biblical studies, exegesis, and interpretation, and also tend to be more open to the development of the social and psychological sciences, including studies in crime and penology, more than their conservative religious friends.

When it comes to capital punishment, the Hebrew Bible—the Old Testament—speaks in multiple voices. The Bible's primordial murder story—the slaying of Abel by his brother Cain—ends with God forbidding capital punishment. God "set a mark upon Cain, lest any finding him should kill him," and decrees that "whosoever slayeth Cain, vengeance shall be taken on him sevenfold."

Yet many scriptures can be cited to boost the religious belief that capital punishment is demanded, sanctioned by, or is at least acceptable to God. One classic example comes just a few chapters after the story of Cain: "If anyone sheds the blood of man, by man shall his blood be shed; for in the image of God has man been made" (Genesis 9:6).

Exodus 21:12–17: "Anyone who strikes a man and so causes his death, must die. If he has not lain in wait for him but God has delivered him into his hands, then I will appoint you a place where he may seek refuge. But should a man dare to kill his fellow by treacherous intent, you must take him even from my altar to be put to death. Anyone who abducts a man—whether he has sold him or is found in possession of him—must die. Anyone who curses father or mother must die."

Exodus 21:23–25: ". . . but should she die, you shall give life for life, eye for eye, tooth for tooth, hand for hand, foot for foot, burn for burn, wound for wound, stroke for stroke." (This is known as the law of *lex talionis,* or "an eye for an eye and a tooth for a tooth." It is usually misunderstood and interpreted as vengeful. However, that was not its intent. Its real intent was to set limits—to make sure that the payment did not exceed the debt actually incurred.)

Exodus 21:28–29: "When an ox gores a man or woman to death, the ox must be stoned. Its flesh shall not be eaten, and the owner of the ox shall not be liable. But if the ox has been in the habit of goring before, and if its owner was warned but has not kept it under control, then should this ox kill a man or woman, the ox must be stoned and its owner put to death."

Exodus 22:18: "Anyone who has intercourse with an animal must die."

Leviticus 20:2: "Tell the sons of Israel: Any son of Israel or any stranger living in Israel must die if he hands over any of his children to Molech."

Leviticus 20:10–16: "The man who commits adultery with a married woman; the man who commits adultery with his neighbor's wife must die, he and his accomplice. The man who lies with his father's wife has uncovered his father's nakedness. Both of them must die, their blood shall be on their own heads. The man who lies with his daughter-in-law; both of them must die; they have defiled each other, their blood shall be on their own heads."

Leviticus 20:27: "Any man or woman who is a necromancer or magician must be put to death by stoning; their blood shall be on their own heads."

From these brief readings, one can see that capital punishment was permitted for numerous offenses in ancient Hebrew law, including, but not limited to, murder, kidnapping, selling a person into slavery, adultery, incest, bestiality, and witchcraft. During war, even more drastic measures were permitted against a defeated enemy. Scholars tell us that of Mosaic law's 36 capital offenses, 18 prescribed death by stoning, 10 by burning, 2 by decapitation, and 6 by strangulation.

While most religious conservatives would not argue that we should apply the death penalty to all of the "crimes" cited in the Old Testament, many would argue that the scriptures do permit, and God does sanction, capital punishment for certain heinous crimes.

Yet as has already been pointed out, both Jewish and Christian sages have differed profoundly over how literally to take these directives. According to religious historians and archaeologists, in ancient Israel many if not most of these laws were honored in the breach: designed as statements of a cultural value rather than a statute to be literally enforced. Or, as in the case of Genesis 9:6, more of a proverb than a direct statute—like "he who lives by the sword shall die by the sword." If all of these declarations were ever interpreted literally, notes religious historian Megivern, "the streets of the community would run red with blood, the populace would be slaughtered by its own courts. There is little evidence that ancient Israel was ever such a sanguinary society."

Unlike the Hebrew Bible, the New Testament says nothing

directly about capital punishment. But there are those who argue that there are scriptures that indirectly support state-sponsored execution. One of the most often cited is from Paul's writings, Romans 13:1–3:

> Let every soul be subject unto the higher powers. For there is no power but of God, the powers that be are ordained of God. Whosoever therefore resisteth the power, resisteth the ordinance of God; and they shall receive unto themselves damnation. For the rulers are not a terror to good works, but to the evil.

This scripture is used to legitimize civil governments, including justifying their various functions, such as taxing the people to support government programs, serving in the military to defend the country, and capital punishment to deter crime and protect society. Supporters of the death penalty also cite the fact that when Jesus was tried and sentenced to die, and even when he was actually on the cross, he never once protested or challenged the government's authority to practice capital punishment.

Opponents of the death penalty cite the lack of any justification of capital punishment or a defense of it in the New Testament. If the New Testament does not mandate it, goes this particular argument, then it should not be practiced. Opponents often use the following verses to shore up their position:

Matthew 22:17–21: "Tell us your opinion, then. Is it permissible to pay taxes to Caesar or not? But Jesus was aware of their malice and replied, You hypocrites! Why do you set this trap for me? Let me see the money you pay the tax with. They handed him a denarius, and he said, Whose head is this? Whose name? Caesar's they replied. He then said to them, Very well, give back to Caesar what belongs to Caesar—and to God what belongs to God."

Matthew 5:25–26: "Come to terms with your opponent in good time while you are still on the way to the court with him, or he may hand you over to the judge and the judge to the officer, and you will be thrown into prison. I tell you solemnly, you will not get out till you have paid the last penny."

I Peter 2:13–14: "For the sake of the Lord, accept the authority of every social institution; the emperor, as the supreme authority, and the governors as commissioned by him to punish criminals and praise good citizenship."

Acts 5:29–30: "In reply Peter and the apostles said, Obedience to God comes before obedience to men; it was the God of our ancestors who raised up Jesus, but it was you who had him executed by hanging on a tree."

Titus 3:1: "Remind them that it is their duty to be obedient to the officials and representatives of the government."

Romans 13:3–4: "Good behavior is not afraid of magistrates; only criminals have anything to fear. If you want to live without being afraid of authority, you must live honestly and authority may even honor you."

Romans 13:6–7: "This is also the reason why you must pay taxes, since all government officials are God's officers. They serve God by collecting taxes. Pay every government official what he has a right to ask—whether it be direct tax or indirect, fear or honor."

And, of course, John 8:3–11: "The scribes and Pharisees brought a woman along who had been caught committing adultery; and making her stand there in full view of everybody, they said to Jesus, Master, this woman was caught in the very act of committing adultery, and Moses has ordered us in the Law to condemn

103

women like this to death by stoning. What have you to say? They asked him this as a test, looking for something to use against him. But Jesus bent down and started writing on the ground with his finger. As they persisted with their question, he looked up and said, If there is one of you who has not sinned, let him be the first to throw a stone at her. Then he bent down and wrote on the ground again. When they heard this they went away one by one, beginning with the eldest, until Jesus was left alone with the woman, who remained standing there. He looked up and said, Woman, where are they? Has no one condemned you? No one, sir, she replied. Neither do I condemn you, said Jesus. Go away, and don't sin any more."

And what about the Fifth Commandment? The Fifth Commandment, of course, is "Thou shalt not kill." Read literally, that should theologically settle the question of the justness of the death penalty. It does not. Historically, there have been three exceptions to the Fifth Commandment—three types of killing—acceptable by churches and theologians: killing in the context of conducting a "just war"; killing in self-defense; and our subject, killing in the form of capital punishment to protect society.

If nothing else, this exercise shows the limitations of "proof-texting" as an answer to the death-penalty debate. The Bible, like the communities of faith that draw upon it and the societies in which they live, speaks on many sides of the question. But whatever may be the human, humane, or societal objections to capital punishment, Judeo-Christian opposition begins with the premise that God is the creator and human beings are the creatures. From this religious viewpoint, life is not accidental; it is providential. Life is sacred. Therefore, other human beings do not have the right, and should not be given the power, to take away what God has created.

PSALMS 8:3–5:

I look up at your heavens, made by your fingers,

at the moon and stars you set in place—

ah, what is man that you should spare a thought for him,

the son of man that you should care for him?

Yet you have made him little less than a god (or the angels)

you have crowned him with glory and splendor

If God created each human being a "little less than the angels," then all life—even the life of a guilty criminal, one who did not treat other lives as sacred, a human being who has gone astray—is sacred, must be revered, and must be treated with dignity and respect. Even the criminal has certain God-given human rights—the right to a fair judicial process and to fair and humane punishment that fits the crime.

That does not mean that the rights or the plight of the victims of crime are not protected, preserved, and honored. It simply means that the rights and the dignity of all human beings—victims and victimizers—must be respected and protected. It is understandable that the victims of crime (and their families and loved ones) might not feel this way. That is why a dispassionate and just society, and the law, must at times intervene—to preserve the rights and dignity of all concerned.

From a Judeo-Christian perspective, appropriate punishment must answer several questions and pass several tests.

First, what is the purpose of the punishment? Its purpose must be twofold: to reform the individual and to achieve retribution—

to make the person pay a just price for the crime. Obviously, capital punishment eliminates the first, for a dead person cannot be reformed or rehabilitated. The second raises the question of proportionality, or fitting the punishment to the crime. Are the means limited to achieving the just end? Are the means in proportion to the just end?

Second, what are the motives of those doing the punishing? From a Judeo-Christian perspective, vindictive and vengeful motives are unacceptable: "Vengeance is mine saith the Lord." If the motive of punishment is pure, then a person who committed a crime because he was mentally or emotionally sick or socially scarred would be incarcerated, treated, and rehabilitated, not executed. If he were fully responsible for the crime, he would be incarcerated—punished in proportion to the crime—and rehabilitated (if possible), not executed. If rehabilitation were impossible, and a judgment is made that the criminal is incapable of self-restraint and would commit further crimes and would further endanger other citizens and society, then life in prison without chance of parole would both prevent further crime and protect society.

Third, how effective is the punishment? Some state that capital punishment is the lesser of two evils—that the state must kill certain criminals in order to safeguard society by deterring other individuals from committing the same crimes. If that is the argument, then the burden of proof falls on those who support it to show conclusive proof not only that the death penalty deters crime but also that it is a necessary deterrent. As discussed earlier in this book, there is no valid evidence indicating that capital punishment is a deterrent.

Fourth, in a slightly broader dimension, is the question of due respect for the decent opinion of humanity. World opinion increasingly stands against capital punishment. More and more governments are outlawing its use, and more and more religious leaders are speaking out against the practice. On the terrain of capital punishment, the United States now is aligned with governments we otherwise dismiss as "rogue" states. We are one of only six nations that execute minors. The rest of the Judeo-Christian world is moving away from capital punishment as a way of dealing with crime and criminality. It is time for us—as part of those same faith traditions—to join them.

CHAPTER 8

A Society of

Executioners

"I was just working in the shop, then all of a sudden
something just triggered in me and I started shaking
and I walked back into the house, and my wife asked
'what's the matter,' and I said, 'I don't feel good,' and
tears, uncontrollable tears, was coming out of my eyes.
And she said, 'what's the matter,' and I said, 'I just
thought about that execution two days ago, and everybody else's that I was involved with.' . . . You see, I can
barely even talk because I'm thinking more and more
of it, you know. There was just so many of them."
—FRED ALLEN, FORMER HUNTSVILLE,
ALABAMA, CORRECTIONAL OFFICER
AND PARTICIPANT IN 120 EXECUTIONS

We know what the death penalty doesn't do. We know from scientific research that capital punishment does not deter crime or
make America safer. We know the death penalty is not meting out

balanced justice to black and white, rich and poor. We know executions are not providing closure to victims, and are not meting out some universal theological mandate. We know that capital sentences do not even reflect a consensus among Americans about how the law should be applied, since only the firmest supporters of the death penalty are allowed to serve on capital juries, effectively insulating trials from doubt.

But the question then remains: What *is* the death penalty doing to America?

Some answers to that question are easy to quantify or assess. For instance:

- Capital punishment is costing American taxpayers a great deal of money. Of course, the death penalty would raise moral questions even if it were cost-effective. But the reality—which concerns a growing number of governors and legislators—is that the special housing required for death-row inmates, the detailed reinvestigations needed to establish claims of innocence, the years of appeals, the high-tech lethal-injection equipment and execution chambers, all are expensive. The Death Penalty Information Center estimates that each executed prisoner costs more than $1.5 million from trial to killing, compared with $18,000 per year for incarcerating a non–death row inmate.

- Capital punishment, putting the United States in the dubious human-rights company of Iran, Iraq, China, and Saudi Arabia, is hurting America's relationship with our neighbors and allies. Eighty-seven foreign nationals currently reside on American death rows, 46 of them from Mexico, where American executions are a raw emotional issue. Germany is currently suing the United States in the World Court, seeking reparations for the executions of Karl and Walter LaGrand in Arizona in 1999.

In years on death row, these two German nationals were never advised of their right to seek aid from their nation's consulate. American executions are routinely front-page news in Europe, and France—which abolished the guillotine in 1981—made campaigning against the American death penalty a central focus of its presidency of the European Union in 2000. A growing number of nations—including Canada, France, and Israel—are refusing to extradite criminal suspects to the United States if they might face execution. Mary Robinson, the United Nations High Commissioner for Human Rights and former president of Ireland, has denounced U.S. capital punishment as running "counter to widely accepted international principles," and condemns in the strongest terms the executions of inmates like Gary Graham for crimes alleged to have been committed while still a juvenile.

• The rising number of death-row innocence cases, and the massive racial and class inequality of capital trials, is eroding rather than enhancing public confidence in the justice system. A Roper poll of Illinois residents conducted in late 2000 found that three-quarters of that state's residents believe innocent individuals have been executed. This is not only a stunning reappraisal of the politics of death, but an indicator that most people think the criminal-justice system is not to be trusted to protect the innocent.

But some effects of capital punishment are more subtle—and, perhaps, more disturbing. Take the widespread clamor for a public telecast of Timothy McVeigh's execution. The call to make McVeigh's lethal injection into a public spectacle surfaced in some decidedly mainstream quarters. In *The New York Times,* for instance, poet and essayist Thomas Lynch wrote of the public's "unabridged right" to watch McVeigh die. Lynch called public broadcast of the execution "a vaccination against madness and inhumanity." Ironically, those calls were echoed by McVeigh himself, who wanted his execution shown on national television. This tortuous debate shows why any thought that McVeigh's execution represented "closure" was badly mistaken. Instead of recalling McVeigh's victims or encouraging violence prevention, most of the press and pundits spent the spring of 2001 talking about how big a crowd would watch McVeigh get poison dripped into his veins. Would it be a national TV audience, or only 200 Oklahoma City survivors? Instead of fading into the anonymity of life behind bars, McVeigh was able to keep himself on the front page, to tease reporters with promises of execution-eve interviews, to turn the chronicle of his last months on earth into a testament for the militia fringe.

The proposition that public broadcast of executions is some kind of therapy is not a proposition supported by scholarship. To the contrary, a growing number of psychologists believe that broadcast images of killing help desensitize viewers to their own moral qualms, creating what psychologist David Grossman, a former lieutenant colonel in the Army Rangers and a national authority on what makes it possible for people to kill, calls "a new cult of vengeance." As Grossman has written, television and movie audiences easily learn to associate images of inflicted death with "entertainment, pleasure, their favorite soft drink, their favorite candy bar and the close, intimate contact of their date." And what they remember, even when the bad guys get their just deserts, is not the law but the vengeance. Indeed, Lt. Col. Grossman says, McVeigh's bombing itself exemplifies this "new cult of vengeance." The macabre clamor for a public spectacle means that in the end, McVeigh can twist his own execution as just another exercise in vengeance against a corrupt system.

Grossman's contention that killing desensitizes the public is borne out by rarely seen photos of the last public execution in the United States. It was 1936 in Owensboro, Kentucky. Rainey Bethea, a 22-year-old black man, was hanged for assaulting and murdering an elderly white woman. The photos show an all-white crowd of 10,000 to 20,000 people, in their Sunday best and straw hats, chatting amiably as Bethea's hooded body dangles above the trap.

There is in fact some scholarship that suggests that the violence of officially sponsored state executions brutalizes the sensibilities of society and actually increases the murder rate by loosening the inhibitions of potential murderers and offering the example of sanctioned vengeance. While academic studies conflict on this point, and violence has many causes, it's certainly the case that the state with the highest execution rate—Texas—has a higher violent crime rate than New York, and the cities of Texas together with those of Florida have resisted the steep national decline in crime.

Today's executions are exercises in the engineering of death, the institutionalizing of death, the bureaucratizing of death. Every technological "improvement" in execution broadens the circle of complicity for killing, and at the same time allows those who participate to deny that an act of violence is taking place. "Being [a] former farmer and horse raiser, I know what it's like to try and eliminate an injured horse by shooting him," Governor Ronald Reagan of California said in 1973, envisioning instead "a simple shot or tranquilizer." The goal, in Reagan's view, was not to spare the defendant pain but to spare the executioner—and by extension the rest of us—anguish. "I think and I hope that this will provide some dignity with death," another governor, Thomas Brisco of Texas, said as he signed his own state's lethal-injection bill.

Where once a single hangman pulled the trap, today's death penalty enlists engineers to design high-tech lethal-injection pumps, pharamacists to distribute poison rather than medicine, medical teams to kill rather than heal. Journalists are enlisted in the routine. At Huntsville, Texas, there are newspaper reporters who have witnessed as many as 170 killings. Guards assigned to so-called tie-down teams are expected to assist with killing, then go home to their spouses and children, dozens of times a year. Given this degree of moral disconnect, it is perhaps worth pondering that the inventor of the lethal-injection apparatus now used on most death rows was Dr. Thomas Leuchtner, a Holocaust denier.

Law, too, is compromised by the rush for finality over fairness. The whole arc of Supreme Court decisions about the death penalty since 1975 has been to make capital justice less fair, less open to appeal. It is as if the Supreme Court has thrown up its hands and admitted that the only way to have the death penalty is to accept racism, to accept sleeping lawyers and drunk lawyers, to accept the execution of the innocent in the package.

As the pace of execution rises, capital punishment is also emerging as a great test of American political leadership. Capital punishment has long tested the willingness of leaders to resist the politically expedient. In the early 1890s, Illinois governor John Peter Altgeld became convinced that eight anarchists had been wrongfully convicted of throwing a bomb during an 1886 labor rally (the so-called Haymarket Riot) in which eight police officers were killed. Four of the defendants had already been hanged and one committed suicide, but Altgeld pardoned the three remaining survivors in 1893—even though he knew it would be the end of his political career. Altgeld was voted out of office and hounded until his death as "John Pardon Altgeld."

In our own time, the intense politics of the death penalty can turn honorable leaders into pretzels. When George W. Bush mocked Karla Faye Tucker and executed Gary Graham despite widespread doubt of his guilt, he failed that test; so did Bill Clinton, when as governor of Arkansas he executed brain-damaged Rickie Ray Rector. Governor Mario Cuomo of New York made a different decision in 1994, risking hurting his chances at reelection rather than abandoning his opposition to New York reinstating its death penalty.

Governor George Ryan of Illinois faced the same leadership test in 1999, when he took office on the heels of the exoneration of 13 Illinois death-row inmates. Ryan's answer—a statewide moratorium on executions—received international attention, but his journey to that decision remained a largely private matter. He did not make the decision in a vacuum—legislators, lawyers, and the media played a big role—but what led him to break so definitively with the bipartisan pro-execution consensus, and where his thinking has gone since, strikes at the core of the shifting politics of death.

Ryan, whose family owned several neighborhood drugstores in Kankakee for 40 years, joined the Illinois legislature in the 1970s as a staunch law-and-order man. "I believed some crimes were so heinous that the only proper way of protecting society was execution. I saw a nation in the grip of increasing crime rates; and tough sentences, more jails, the death penalty—that was good government." In 1977, after the Supreme Court lifted its ban on execution, a bill to reinstate the death penalty came before the statehouse in Springfield. When an anti–death penalty legislator asked his colleagues to consider whether they personally would be willing to throw the switch, Ryan rose to his feet with "unequivocal words of support" for execution—words he now regrets. The truth, though, was that Ryan never thought about capital punishment much, before that vote or for more than 20 years afterward, except as an abstract idea of justice. "I supported the death penalty, I believed in the death penalty, I voted for the death penalty."

In September 1998, as Ryan was running for governor, Anthony Porter, with his 51 IQ, was scheduled for death. Two days before Porter's execution date his lawyers won a temporary reprieve, Northwestern University journalism professor David Protess turned his investigative-reporting students loose on the case, and by February the evidence they obtained left the newly inaugurated Governor Ryan reeling: a videotaped confession by the real killer that led to the freeing of Porter after eighteen years. "I was caught completely off guard. Maybe I shouldn't have been, but I was. That mentally retarded man came within two days of execution, and but for those students Anthony Porter would have been dead and buried. I felt jolted into reexamining everything I believed in." At first, a conflicted Ryan waffled on a full-fledged review of Illinois' capital apparatus, but ultimately he endorsed one concrete initiative: an $18 million capital-crimes litigation fund to ensure that defendants like Porter, as well as prosecutors, have access to investigative resources.

That experience also collided, within weeks, with a gubernatorial responsibility Ryan himself had helped enact: signing off on an execution. In the spring of 1999 the case of Andrew Kokoraleis landed on Ryan's desk. Kokoraleis had been found guilty of the rape, mutilation, and murder of a 21-year-old woman. "This was a horrible crime, and I am the father of five daughters. But after the mistakes the system had made with Porter, I wasn't sure what to do. I agonized. I checked and double-checked and triple-checked the facts." In the end Ryan went through with it, and Kokoraleis was executed. But, says Ryan, "it was the most emotional experience I have ever been through in my life. It all came down to me—the one fellow who has to pull the switch. Quite frankly, that is too much to ask of one person."

Within three months, two more Illinois death-row inmates were exonerated: one by DNA evidence, the other when a jail-house informant's testimony was discredited. The state judiciary began its own investigation, and the calls for a moratorium grew. Still, said Ryan, "I was resisting." But one day "the attorney general called seeking a new execution date for an inmate. In my heart at that moment, I couldn't go forward with it." Political cynics wondered if Ryan shifted his position to deflect attention from charges of corruption against his secretary of state, but Ryan's description of his internal turmoil is compelling. "I knew I couldn't make myself live through what I'd experienced with Kokoraleis," he says. "I just couldn't do it again."

In the fall of 1999 the *Chicago Tribune* published an examination of every Illinois death-row case since 1977, revealing, among other things, that more than one-third of all 285 Illinois capital convictions over that period had been reversed because of "fundamental error." It was the final straw. In January 2000 Ryan acted, unilaterally issuing his moratorium. He also assembled a commission, including such notable death-penalty opponents as attorney and best-selling author Scott Turow and former senator Paul Simon, to report on the roots of Illinois' false-conviction record.

In the time since his moratorium, Ryan's position has evolved further. At first, he told Northwestern students he doubted there would be another execution on his watch. Now, he is convinced that "moral certainty" in capital cases isn't possible. And he's broadened his focus: "My concern is not just with the death penalty as a singular issue; it's with the entire criminal-justice system. If innocent people are sentenced to death—cases that get all kinds of scrutiny—what does that say about invisible, low-level cases, drug cases and so on?"

Ryan argues, with great passion, that criminal-justice reformers need to extend their traditional concern for the poor to middle-class and suburban defendants—building a bridge to new constituencies. "I have seen people charged in drug cases where down comes the full force of the federal Treasury," he says. "Someone who is poor will get a free lawyer. But a truck driver, for instance, will have to mortgage his house and sell his rig to pay a lawyer. Then, when he is found not guilty, where can he go to get that house back, to get on with his life?"

Ryan's transformation is a journey still in progress. Most Americans will never have the occasion to feel revulsion for their own role in an execution. But that "jolt" he felt, and the moral anguish that followed, mirror a growing public unease. "A lot of people are like me, I think. The death penalty was a fact of life," he says. "But as people become more and more aware of the unfairness, they become less enthusiastic." Ryan, the heartland conservative, has tested his lifelong support for the death penalty against the evidence, and the institution has come up short: "I question the entire system and the people connected with it."

CHAPTER 9

The Death Penalty and America's Future:

Moratorium and Beyond

"I will no longer tinker with the machinery of death."
—JUSTICE HARRY BLACKMUN,
CALLINS v. *COLLINS*, 1994

It is clear that ever more Americans feel trapped by capital punishment—just as trapped as Governor Ryan before he stepped forward and said "enough." While our ultimate philosophical conclusions about capital punishment may still differ, both "traditional" death-penalty abolitionists and longtime death-penalty supporters are trapped by a system that has resulted in nearly 100 mistaken death sentences. We feel trapped by the profound economic inequities and racism of capital justice, by the rapid pace of execution in a few states, by the inflexibility and lack of compassionate leadership reflected in the executions of a Karla Faye Tucker or Gary Graham. The polls show this unease among the American people as a whole; the media reflect it among figures such as columnist George Will, former FBI director William Sessions, and Pat Robertson.

Is there a way out of the death-penalty trap? Yes. The simple fact is that it is time for a national time-out on execution—a moratorium like the one ordered in Illinois by Governor Ryan in 2000, or like the time-out on executions imposed by Maryland's Supreme Court in the spring of 2001.

A death-penalty moratorium is not abolition of capital punishment—nor is it the end of the national conversation about the death penalty. To the contrary. A moratorium is needed if that conversation is ever to take place.

The need for such a conversation is clear. The frequency of death-row exonerations and the vast inequities of the capital-trial system would be reason enough. But there is also an important political reality. There is today no national consensus about capital punishment. It is not just opinion polls that show the country profoundly divided. The same fault lines are visible in every branch of government. In 1976 Justice Lewis Powell writing for the Supreme Court majority in *Gregg* v. *Georgia* said that numerous initiatives by state legislatures to reintroduce capital punishment were evidence of widespread public support. But today, state legislatures are themselves pressing moratorium legislation, new limitations on execution, and capital-trial reform; in early 2000 the legislature of conservative New Hampshire outright repealed its death penalty. City councils representing millions of Americans are demanding that executions be halted. In 1976, seven Supreme Court justices voted to reinstate executions. Two of them—Blackmun and Powell himself—swiftly came to regret their votes. Today's Supreme Court—comprised entirely of justices named by pro–death penalty presidents—routinely splits 5–4 in death cases. Justice Ruth Bader Ginsburg, an avowed death-penalty supporter when she was named in 1994, in 2000 endorsed a proposed moratorium on execution in Maryland. The point is simple: The national consensus cited by the Supreme Court in *Gregg* no longer exists—not among the public, and not in the federal judiciary.

In Illinois, Governor Ryan appointed a commission to study whether the conditions that led to the near executions of 13 innocent individuals could ever be remedied. That commission included both pro– and anti–capital punishment advocates. A national moratorium would provide an opportunity for Congress and courts to appoint a commission to ask hard policy questions, without the atmosphere of intense emotion surrounding every additional execution.

America has already had one effective death-penalty moratorium—the ten years from 1967 to 1977 when a variety of judicial decisions leading up to *Furman* v. *Georgia* brought executions to a halt. But the current drive for a moratorium is different, since it relies not upon a few appointed justices but upon the people's representatives—governors, state legislatures, and Congress. The current drive for a moratorium really began in Illinois in 1996, when a state legislator proposed a moratorium bill and exonerated death-row inmate Delbert Tibbs bicycled the state to call attention to the issue.

The idea of a national moratorium gained momentum with a resolution passed by the American Bar Association, the largest association of lawyers in the country, in 1997. The ABA explicitly refused to take a position for or against the death penalty. Instead, the ABA found that, in the words of its president, Anthony Amsterdam, "Whatever one's views about capital punishment in the abstract, there are compelling reasons to believe that the way it is practiced in the United States today is fatally unjust and prone to error." The ABA cited three reasons for a national time-out: the failure of states to guarantee effective lawyers in death cases; the stripping of death-row inamtes' rights to appeal; and "long-standing patterns of racial discrimination, which, the ABA says, have poisoned capital justice.

In May of 2001, President Bush and Attorney General John Ashcroft delayed the execution of Oklahoma City bomber Timothy McVeigh. They did so because it turned out that thousands of pages of FBI documents had never been turned over to McVeigh's defense team. Even though McVeigh had confessed to the bombing, President Bush and Attorney General Ashcroft recognized a fundamental principle: new evidence, official malfeasance, and legal uncertainty all demand a "time-out" on execution to investigate unresolved questions.

Yet it is clear that the precise issues that led to that time-out in McVeigh's execution riddle death cases nationwide. If thousands of pages of evidence could be "lost" in the FBI's back drawer, in the worst act of domestic terrorism in American history and the first federal execution in nearly 40 years, what does that say about less visible cases and less well-equipped law-enforcement agencies? If a time-out, however long or short, was justified in the single case of Timothy McVeigh, does not the accumulated record of lost evidence, law-enforcement misconduct, mistaken eyewitness identification, and outright factual innocence demand a systematic and definitive time-out on all executions?

A moratorium would address what is unquestionably an escalating national crisis of confidence in criminal justice. Nearly 100 exonerated death-row inmates amounts to a crisis not just for capital punishment but for the whole judicial system. A moratorium, accompanied by a serious commission of inquiry, would be a forward-looking acknowledgment of this widespread public alarm. A moratorium, in short, would begin the process of holding the capital-punishment system accountable.

A moratorium would also enable the country to confront one of the big lies of the death-penalty debate: that the American public holds an "absolute" and inflexible opinion on capital punishment. This myth—the idea that the country is made up of permanently warring liberals and conservatives, with no possibility of common ground—serves politicians who can pander to one constituency or another, and it serves the news media, which can oversimplify complex issues. But it ignores a central fact of the death-penalty debate: In the presence of new information, people change their minds. Governor Ryan, long a death-penalty supporter, changed his mind when confronted with the facts; Justices Powell and Blackmun, two Republican appointees who voted to reinstate executions in 1976, both changed their minds by the end of their lives; evangelical Christians shocked by Karla Faye Tucker's execution changed their minds as well.

Considering the profound moral and legal questions involved in capital punishment, scholarship on why people think what they do about executions is surprisingly scant. Fear of crime may have something to do with people supporting the death penalty, but that may not be everything. Homicide rates were rising, after all, during the death-penalty nadir of the late 1960s. In the mid-1970s, social psychologist Lawrence Kohlberg theorized that then low levels of support for the death penalty indicated that America had passed to a new stage of moral development. Within a few years the numbers were escalating again; so much for Kohlberg's optimistic theory.

The most substantive look at the public's death-penalty decision making has come from criminologist Robert Bohm. After tracking a study sample's shifting views in the early 1990s, he came to two seemingly simple conclusions: The more information people have about the death penalty, the less likely they are to support it; and when people change their position on capital punishment, it is not because they reject the premise of execution. Instead, it is because of doubts about the death-penalty's administration, especially about false conviction, racial discrimination, and other questions of fairness.

Events of recent years bear out Bohm's theory. When Justice Blackmun declared in 1994 that he would no longer "tinker with the machinery of death," it was not because of any newfound moral absolutism. Rather, he said, looking up close and personal at dozens of death cases convinced him that there is no way "to prevent the more subtle and often unconscious forms of racism from creeping into the system." Young black males, he believed, would always be vulnerable to unjust execution. So would the poor of all races. Economic and racial inequity, he learned, "could not be purged from the administration of capital punishment without sacrificing the equally essential component of fairness—individualized sentencing."

The historic Illinois moratorium was also, ultimately, the result of the public getting more information. In this case, it was through the work of writers and investgative reporters. First, to those journalism students at Northwestern University, who in recent years freed a half-dozen wrongly convicted death-row inmates; then to author Scott Turow, who proved the innocence of an inmate who came within two weeks of execution; and, most recently, to the devastating and comprehensive investigative reporting of the *Chicago Tribune*, revealing a Kafkaesque parade of disbarred defense attorneys, lying prosecutors, bad forensic science, and all-white juries. What, finally, has shifted public perception? Not the moral position of convinced abolitionists, surely, a position un-changed for decades. Instead it was stories and information—sto-ries and information that are too easily drowned out by the intense emotion surrounding executions.

In some respects, a national moratorium would be as pro-foundly challenging to death-penalty abolitionists as to death-penalty supporters. Strategically and philosphically, it will demand that abolitionists look beyond the moratorium to building a broad public constituency for a new approach to criminal justice.

For one thing, pro-execution forces could easily use a morato-rium to buy time until the public's current outrage has cooled. The philosopher and historian Hugo Adam Bedau notes that throughout American history proponents of capital punishment have often dulled calls for abolition with a few token legal reforms, such as the creation of degrees of murder in Pennsylvania in the early nineteenth century. "The dominant (if often tacit) concern of the defenders of capital punishment," Bedau writes, has been "to shape the law and the administration of the death penalty so as to winnow the worst offenders . . . and so, by this compromise, to prevent the complete abolition of capital punishment."

In order to build support to make a moratorium permanent, death-penalty abolitionists would be forced to listen carefully to the public's fears about violent crime, and consider whether to en-courage narrowly cast life sentences without parole as an alterna-tive to execution. Life sentences without parole are a hard pill for many death-penalty abolitionists—a true life sentence means giv-ing up on the possibility of rehabilitation and ignoring the fact that few offenders commit violent crime late in life. Yet every opin-ion poll suggests that the public's support for capital punishment falls most dramatically if they are confident in the security of life sentences.

In fact, two case studies demonstrate the effectiveness of life without parole—at least in the cases of a small, narrowly defined number of very dangerous offenders—as a meaningful, practical alternative to the death penalty. In Alabama, life without the possibility of parole has been met with praise, where it is seen not only as an alternative to the death penalty but also as a more efficient means of sentencing. Prosecutors welcome another choice when attempting to secure a plea bargain or when trying capital cases because of the public's perception that a "regular" life sentence is too lenient. Having this extra weapon of life without parole means prosecutors do not have to pursue the death penalty as the only alternative to letting a convicted murderer walk free.

Alabama has also had a generally positive experience with the behavior of the prison "lifers." In fact, a study of the Alabama prison system reveals that prisoners sentenced to life without the possibility of parole "commit 50 percent fewer disciplinary offenses per capita than all others combined."

This revelation is confirmed in other states. In Michigan, "lifers" have proven to be some of the most disciplined prisoners. To fight the system for 25 or more years, they realize, is useless. Leo Lalonde, a Michigan Department of Corrections official, observes that "After a few years, lifers become your better prisoners. They tend to adjust and just do their time. They tend to be a calming influence on the younger kids, and we have more problems with people serving short terms."

While Alabama offers only two choices in the most serious capital cases, Kentucky's justice system is notable for the flexibility it gives to prosecutors, defenders, and those handing down sentences. In 1986 the Kentucky legislature passed the Truth in Sentencing Act in order to lengthen the time violent offenders—especially murderers—spend behind bars. They added to the existing statutes the option of a minimum term of 25 years without parole, which sentence would run longer than the standard life sentence. This is tougher than a regular life sentence, but does not carry the finality of capital punishment.

Kentucky's prosecutors now have a whole range of sentences to pursue, allowing them to truly make the punishment fit the crime. Besides the death penalty, they can choose life without the possibility of parole, life without the possibility of parole for 25 years, or a regular life sentence. Juries and judges also can tailor their sentences more accurately to the individual crime. The system is also popular with the state's citizens, who sought tougher sentencing.

Looking beyond a moratorium also means looking beyond the death penalty. It means recognition that the system of state killing—and the systematic stripping away of death-row inmates' rights since 1975—is only one central element of the much larger prison-industrial complex. Confronting the death penalty ultimately means confronting mandatory-minimum sentences, three-strikes laws, the drug war, and privatized prisons. In 1976, the year that the Supreme Court reinstated capital punishment in *Gregg* v. *Georgia,* the nation's incarcerated population stood at just 200,000. Today, it is 2 million. We live in the Age of Incarceration, as surely as the Great Depression defined the 1930s and the civil rights revolution and Vietnam configured the 1960s. A death-penalty moratorium is just one step in addressing the fundamental shift in American life, a shift that has left one-third of young African-American males—and hundreds of thousands of others—behind bars.

Looking beyond a moratorium also means imagining a new death-penalty abolitionism that meets Americans not only on the ground of moral absolutes but also at their alarm about innocence and inequity. Such a new abolitionism, too, must engage a broader swath of churches and community institutions. Sadly, the eloquent statements of clergy opposed to capital punishment have only rarely been matched by proactive enagement with the issue: congregations adopting death-row inmates, pressing elected prosecutors and judges to distance themselves from capital punishment, and otherwise bearing constant witness against the death-penalty drumbeat.

On a profound level, today's controversy about the death penalty amounts to nothing less than a constitutional crisis—if by that we mean the public's confidence in the basic machinery of American democracy. In confronting this crisis, it is useful to recall the words of Justice Thurgood Marshall in his opinion in the *Furman* decision in 1972:

> At a time in our history when the streets of the nation's cities inspire fear and despair, rather than pride and hope, it is difficult to maintain objectivity and concern for our fellow citizens. But, the measure of a country's greatness is its ability to retain compassion in time of crisis. No nation in the recorded history of man has a greater tradition of revering justice and fair treatment for all its citizens in times of turmoil, confusion, and tension than ours. This is a country that clings to fundamental principles, cherishes its constitutional heritage, and rejects simple solutions that compromise the values that lie at the roots of our democratic system.
>
> In striking down capital punishment, this Court does not malign our system of government. On the contrary, it pays homage to it. Only in a free society could right triumph in difficult times, and could civilization record its magnificent ad-

vancement. In recognizing the humanity of our fellow beings, we pay ourselves the highest tribute. We achieve "a major milestone in the long road up from barbarism" and join the approximately 70 other jurisdictions in the world which celebrate their regard for civilization and humanity by shunning capital punishment.

As Justice Marshall understood, the death penalty is not just an argument over how to punish a few violent individuals. It is an argument about how America imagines itself: in relationship to our own past, to our Bill of Rights, to our fellow citizens, and to the world. There is a clear choice to be made. We have inherited a death penalty that is a relic, in so many ways, of the worst of the American past. A new American century need not repeat the same mistakes.

AFTERWORD

National Death Penalty

Moratorium Act of 2001

Authors' note: On March 15, 2001, Representative Jesse L. Jackson, Jr., of Illinois, joined by several House colleagues, introduced H. R. 1038, the National Death Penalty Moratorium Act of 2001. This bill would place a moratorium on executions by the federal government and urge the states to do the same, while a National Commission on the Death Penalty reviews the fairness of the imposition of capital punishment. We hope that the issues and approaches outlined in this bill serve as a model for future debate in Congress and in state legislatures.

IN THE HOUSE OF REPRESENTATIVES

March 15, 2001, Mr. JACKSON of Illinois (for himself, Mr. RODRIGUEZ, Mr. CLAY, Mr. HOEFFEL, and Ms. JACKSON-LEE of Texas) introduced the following bill, which was referred to the Committee on the Judiciary:

A BILL to place a moratorium on executions by the Federal

Government and urge the States to do the same, while a National Commission on the Death Penalty reviews the fairness of the imposition of the death penalty.

Be it enacted by the Senate and House of Representatives of the United States of America in Congress assembled.

Section 1. Short Title

This Act may be cited as the "National Death Penalty Moratorium Act of 2001."

Title I—
Moratorium on the Death Penalty

Sec. 101. Findings

Congress makes the following findings:

(1)   GENERAL FINDINGS

(A)   The administration of the death penalty by the Federal Government and the States should be consistent with our Nation's fundamental principles of fairness, justice, equality, and due process.

(B)   At a time when Federal executions are scheduled to recommence, Congress should consider that more than ever Americans are questioning the use of the death penalty and calling for assurances that it be fairly applied. Support for the death penalty has dropped to the lowest level in 19 years. An NBC News/Wall Street Journal Poll revealed that 63 percent of Americans support a suspension of executions until questions of fairness can be addressed.

(C)   Documented unfairness in the Federal system requires
       Congress to act and suspend Federal executions. Addi-
       tionally, substantial evidence of unfairness throughout
       death penalty States justifies further investigation by Con-
       gress.

(2)   ADMINISTRATION OF THE DEATH PENALTY BY THE
       FEDERAL GOVERNMENT

(A)   The fairness of the administration of the Federal death
       penalty has recently come under serious scrutiny, specifi-
       cally raising questions of racial and geographic dispari-
       ties:

(i)   Eighty percent of Federal death row inmates are mem-
       bers of minority groups.
(ii)   A report released by the Department of Justice on Sep-
       tember 12, 2000, found that 80 percent of defendants
       who were charged with death-eligible offenses under
       Federal law and whose cases were submitted by the
       United States attorneys under the Department's death
       penalty decision-making procedures were African Ameri-
       can, Hispanic American, or members of other minority
       groups.
(iii) The Department of Justice report shows that United
       States attorneys in only 5 of 94 Federal districts—1 each
       in Virginia, Maryland, Puerto Rico, and 2 in New York—
       submit 40 percent of all cases in which the death penalty
       is considered.
(iv)   The Department of Justice report shows that United
       States attorneys who have frequently recommended

seeking the death penalty are often from States with a high number of executions under State law, including Texas, Virginia, and Missouri.

(v)   The Department of Justice report shows that white defendants are more likely than black defendants to negotiate plea bargains saving them from the death penalty in Federal cases.

(vi) A study conducted by the House Judiciary Subcommittee on Civil and Constitutional Rights in 1994 concluded that 89 percent of defendants selected for capital prosecution under the Anti-Drug Abuse Act of 1988 were either African American or Hispanic American.

(vii) The National Institute of Justice has already set into motion a comprehensive study of these racial and geographic disparities.

(viii) Federal executions should not proceed until these disparities are fully studied, discussed, and the Federal death penalty process is subjected to necessary remedial action.

(B)   In addition to racial and geographic disparities in the administration of the Federal death penalty, other serious questions exist about the fairness and reliability of Federal death penalty prosecutions:

(i)   Federal prosecutors rely heavily on bargained-for testimony from accomplices of the capital defendant, which is often obtained in exchange for not seeking the death penalty against the accomplices. This practice creates a serious risk of false testimony.

(ii) Federal prosecutors are not required to provide discovery sufficiently ahead of trial to permit the defense to be prepared to use this information effectively in defending their clients.

(iii) The Federal Bureau of Investigation (FBI), in increasing isolation from the rest of the nation's law enforcement agencies, refuses to make electronic recordings of interrogations that produce confessions, thus making subsequent scrutiny of the legality and reliability of such interrogations more difficult.

(iv) Federal prosecutors rely heavily on predictions of "future dangerousness"—predictions deemed unreliable and misleading by the American Psychiatric Association and the American Psychological Association—to secure death sentences.

(3) ADMINISTRATION OF THE DEATH PENALTY BY THE STATES

(A) The punishment of death carries an especially heavy burden to be free from arbitrariness and discrimination. The Supreme Court has held that "super due process," a higher standard than that applied in regular criminal trials, is necessary to meet constitutional requirements. There is significant evidence that States are not providing this heightened level of due process. For example:

(i) In the most comprehensive review of modern death sentencing, Professor James Liebman and researchers at Columbia University found that, during the period 1973 to 1995, 68 percent of all death penalty cases reviewed were overturned due to serious constitutional errors. In the wake of the Liebman study, 6 States (Arizona, Maryland, North Carolina, Illinois, Indiana, and Nebraska), as well as the Chicago Tribune and the Texas Defender Service are conducting additional studies. These studies may expose additional problems. With few exceptions, the rate of error was consistent across all death penalty States.

(ii) Forty percent of the cases overturned were reversed in Federal court after having been upheld by the States.

(B) The high rate of error throughout all death penalty jurisdictions suggests that there is a grave risk that innocent persons may have been, or will likely be, wrongfully executed. Although the Supreme Court has never conclusively addressed the issue of whether executing an innocent person would in and of itself violate the Constitution, in Herrera v. Collins, 506 U.S. 390 (1993), a majority of the court expressed the view that a persuasive demonstration of actual innocence would violate substantive due process rendering imposition of a death sentence unconstitutional. In any event, the wrongful conviction and sentencing of a person to death is a serious concern for many Americans. For example:

(i) After 13 innocent people were released from Illinois death row in the same period that the State had executed 12 people, on January 31, 2000, Governor George Ryan of Illinois imposed a moratorium on executions until he could be "sure with moral certainty that no innocent man or woman is facing a lethal injection, no one will meet that fate."

(ii) Since 1973, 93 persons have been freed and exonerated

from death rows across the country, most after serving lengthy sentences.

(C) Wrongful convictions create a serious public safety problem because the true killer is still at large, while the innocent person languishes in prison.

(D) There are many systemic problems that result in innocent people being convicted such as mistaken identification, reliance on jailhouse informants, reliance on faulty forensic testing and no access to reliable DNA testing. For example:

(i) A study of cases of innocent people who were later exonerated, conducted by attorneys Barry Scheck and Peter Neufeld with "The Innocence Project" at Cardozo Law School, showed that mistaken identifications of eyewitnesses or victims contributed to 84 percent of the wrongful convictions.

(ii) Many persons on death row were convicted prior to 1994 and did not receive the benefit of modern DNA testing. At least 10 individuals sentenced to death have been exonerated through post-conviction DNA testing, some within days of execution. Yet in spite of the current widespread prevalence and availability of DNA testing, many States have procedural barriers blocking introduction of post-conviction DNA testing. More than 30 States have laws that require a motion for a new trial based on newly discovered evidence to be filed within 6 months or less.

(iii) The widespread use of jailhouse snitches who earn reduced charges or sentences by fabricating "admissions" by fellow inmates to unsolved crimes can lead to wrongful convictions.

(iv)   The misuse of forensic evidence can lead to wrongful convictions. A recently released report from the Texas Defender Service entitled "A State of Denial: Texas and the Death Penalty" found 160 cases of official forensic misconduct including 121 cases where expert psychiatrists testified "with absolute certainty that the defendant would be a danger in the future," often without even interviewing the defendant.

(E)   The Sixth Amendment to the Constitution guarantees all accused persons access to competent counsel. The Supreme Court set out standards for determining competency in the case of Strickland v. Washington, 466 U.S. 668 (1984). Unfortunately, there is unequal access to competent counsel throughout death penalty States. For example:

(i)   Ninety percent of capital defendants cannot afford to hire their own attorney.

(ii)   Fewer than one-quarter of the 38 death penalty States have set any standards for competency of counsel and in those few States, these standards were set only recently. In most States, any person who passes a bar examination, even if that attorney has never represented a client in any type of case, may represent a client in a death penalty case.

(iii)   Thirty-seven percent of capital cases were reversed because of ineffective assistance of counsel, according to the Columbia study.

(iv)   The recent Texas report noted problems with Texas defense attorneys who slept through capital trials, ignored obvious exculpatory evidence, suffered discipline for ethical lapses or for being under the influence of drugs or alcohol while representing an indigent capital defendant at trial.

(v)   Poor lawyering was also cited by Governor Ryan in Illinois as a basis for a moratorium. More than half of all capital defendants there were represented by lawyers who were later disciplined or disbarred for unethical conduct.

(F)   The Supreme Court has held that it is a violation of the Eighth Amendment to impose the death penalty in a manner that is arbitrary, capricious, or discriminatory. McCleskey v. Kemp, 481 U.S. 279 (1987). Studies consistently indicate racial disparity in the application of the death penalty both for the defendants and the victims. The death penalty is disparately applied in various regions throughout the country, suggesting arbitrary administration of the death penalty based on where the prosecution takes place. For example:

(i)   Of the 85 executions in the year 2000, 51 percent of the defendants were white, 40 percent were black, 7 percent were Latino and 2 percent Native American. Of the victims in the underlying murder, 76 percent were white, 18 percent were black, 2 percent were Latino, and 3 percent were "other." These figures show a continuing trend since reinstatement of the modern death penalty of a predominance of white victims' cases. Despite the fact that nationally whites and blacks are victims of murder in approximately equal numbers, 83 percent of the victims involved in capital cases overall since reinstatement, and 76 percent of the victims in 2000, have been white. Since this disparity is confirmed in studies that control for similar crimes by defendants with similar backgrounds, it implies that white victims are considered more valuable in the criminal justice system.

(ii) Executions are conducted predominantly in southern States. Ninety percent of all executions in 2000 were conducted in the south. Only 3 States outside the south, Arizona, California, and Missouri, conducted an execution in 2000. Texas accounted for almost as many executions as all the remaining States combined.

Sec. 102. Federal and State Death Penalty Moratorium

(a) IN GENERAL—The Federal Government shall not carry out any sentence of death imposed under Federal law until the Congress considers the final findings and recommendations of the National Commission on the Death Penalty in the report submitted under section 202(c)(2) and the Congress enacts legislation repealing this section and implements or rejects the guidelines and procedures recommended by the Commission.

(b) SENSE OF CONGRESS—It is the sense of Congress that each State that authorizes the use of the death penalty should enact a moratorium on executions to allow time to review whether the administration of the death penalty by that State is consistent with constitutional requirements of fairness, justice, equality, and due process.

Title II—
National Commission on the Death Penalty

Sec. 201. Establishment of Commission

(a)   ESTABLISHMENT—There is established a commission to be known as the National Commission on the Death Penalty (in this title referred to as the "Commission").

(b)   MEMBERSHIP—

(1)   APPOINTMENT—Members of the Commission shall be appointed by the President in consultation with the Attorney General and the Chairmen and Ranking Members of the Committees on the Judiciary of the House of Representatives and the Senate.

(2)   COMPOSITION—The Commission shall be composed of 15 members, of whom—

(A)   3 members shall be Federal or State prosecutors;

(B)   3 members shall be attorneys experienced in capital defense;

(C)   2 members shall be current or former Federal or State judges;

(D)   2 members shall be current or former Federal or State law enforcement officials; and

(E)   5 members shall be individuals from the public or private sector who have knowledge or expertise, whether by experience or training, in matters to be studied by the Commission, which may include—

(i)   officers or employees of the Federal Government or State or local governments;

(ii)   members of academia, nonprofit organizations, the religious community, or industry; and

(iii)   other interested individuals.

(3)   BALANCED VIEWPOINTS—In appointing the members of the Commission, the President shall, to the maximum extent practicable, ensure that the membership of the Commission is fairly balanced with respect to the opinions of the members of the Commission regarding support for or opposition to the use of the death penalty.

(4)   DATE—The appointments of the initial members of the Commission shall be made not later than 30 days after the date of enactment of this Act.

(c)   PERIOD OF APPOINTMENT—Each member shall be appointed for the life of the Commission.

(d)   VACANCIES—A vacancy in the Commission shall not affect the powers of the Commission, but shall be filled in the same manner as the original appointment.

(e)   INITIAL MEETING—Not later than 30 days after all initial members of the Commission have been appointed, the Commission shall hold the first meeting.

(f)   MEETINGS—The Commission shall meet at the call of the Chairperson.

(g)   QUORUM—A majority of the members of the Commission shall constitute a quorum for conducting business, but a lesser number of members may hold hearings.

(h)   CHAIR—The President shall designate 1 member appointed under subsection (a) to serve as the Chair of the Commission.

(i)   RULES AND PROCEDURES—The Commission shall

adopt rules and procedures to govern the proceedings of the Commission.

Sec. 202. Duties of the Commission

(a)   STUDY—

(1)   IN GENERAL—The Commission shall conduct a thorough study of all matters relating to the administration of the death penalty to determine whether the administration of the death penalty comports with constitutional principles and requirements of fairness, justice, equality, and due process.

(2)   MATTERS STUDIED—The matters studied by the Commission shall include the following:

(A)   Racial disparities in capital charging, prosecuting, and sentencing decisions.

(B)   Disproportionality in capital charging, prosecuting, and sentencing decisions based on geographic location and income status of defendants or any other factor resulting in such disproportionality.

(C)   Adequacy of representation of capital defendants, including consideration of the American Bar Association "Guidelines for the Appointment and Performance of Counsel in Death Penalty Cases" (adopted February 1989) and American Bar Association policies that are intended to encourage competency of counsel in capital cases (adopted February 1979, February 1988, February 1990, and August 1996).

(D)   Whether innocent persons have been sentenced to death

and the reasons these wrongful convictions have occurred.

(E) Whether the Federal Government should seek the death
penalty in a State with no death penalty.

(F) Whether courts are adequately exercising independent
judgment on the merits of constitutional claims in State
post-conviction and Federal habeas corpus proceedings.

(G) Whether mentally retarded persons and persons who
were under the age of 18 at the time of their offenses
should be sentenced to death after conviction of death-
eligible offenses.

(H) Procedures to ensure that persons sentenced to death
have access to forensic evidence and modern testing of
forensic evidence, including DNA testing, when modern
testing could result in new evidence of innocence.

(I) Any other law or procedure to ensure that death penalty
cases are administered fairly and impartially, in accordance with the Constitution.

(b) GUIDELINES AND PROCEDURES—

(1) IN GENERAL—Based on the study conducted under
subsection (a), the Commission shall establish guidelines
and procedures for the administration of the death
penalty consistent with paragraph (2).

(2) INTENT OF GUIDELINES AND PROCEDURES—The
guidelines and procedures required by this subsection
shall—

(A) ensure that the death penalty cases are administered
fairly and impartially, in accordance with due process;

(B)   minimize the risk that innocent persons may be executed; and

(C)   ensure that the death penalty is not administered in a racially discriminatory manner.

(c)   REPORT—

(1)   PRELIMINARY REPORT—Not later than 1 year after the date of enactment of this Act, the Commission shall submit to the President, the Attorney General, and the Congress a preliminary report, which shall contain a preliminary statement of findings and conclusions.

(2)   FINAL REPORT—Not later than 2 years after the date of enactment of this Act, the Commission shall submit a report to the President, the Attorney General, and the Congress which shall contain a detailed statement of the findings and conclusions of the Commission, together with the recommendations of the Commission for legislation and administrative actions that implement the guidelines and procedures that the Commission considers appropriate.

Sec. 203. Powers of the Commission

(a)   INFORMATION FROM FEDERAL AND STATE AGENCIES—

(1)   IN GENERAL—The Commission may secure directly from any Federal or State department or agency information that the Commission considers necessary to carry out the provisions of this title.

(2)   FURNISHING OF INFORMATION—Upon a request of the Chairperson of the Commission, the head of any Federal or State department or agency shall furnish the information requested by the Chairperson to the Commission.

(b)   POSTAL SERVICES—The Commission may use the United States mails in the same manner and under the same conditions as other departments and agencies of the Federal Government.

(c)   GIFTS—The Commission may accept, use, and dispose of gifts or donations of services or property.

(d)   HEARINGS—The Commission or, at the direction of the Commission, any subcommittee or member of the Commission, may, for the purpose of carrying out the provisions of this title—

(1)   hold hearings, sit and act at times and places, take testimony, receive evidence, and administer oaths that the Commission, subcommittee, or member considers advisable; and

(2)   require, by subpoena or otherwise, the attendance and testimony of witnesses and the production of books, records, correspondence, memoranda, papers, documents, tapes, and materials that the Commission, subcommittee, or member considers advisable.

(e)   ISSUANCE AND ENFORCEMENT OF SUBPOENAS—

(1)   ISSUANCE—Subpoenas issued pursuant to subsection (d)—

(A)   shall bear the signature of the Chairperson of the Commission; and

(B) shall be served by any person or class of persons designated by the Chairperson for that purpose.

(2) ENFORCEMENT—

(A) IN GENERAL—In the case of contumacy or failure to obey a subpoena issued under subsection (d), the district court of the United States for the judicial district in which the subpoenaed person resides, is served, or may be found, may issue an order requiring that person to appear at any designated place to testify or to produce documentary or other evidence.

(B) CONTEMPT—Any failure to obey a court order issued under subparagraph (A) may be punished by the court as a contempt.

(3) TESTIMONY OF PERSONS IN CUSTODY—A court of the United States within the jurisdiction in which testimony of a person held in custody is sought by the Commission or within the jurisdiction of which such person is held in custody, may, upon application by the Attorney General, issue a writ of habeas corpus ad testificandum requiring the custodian to produce such person before the Commission, or before a member of the Commission or a member of the staff of the Commission designated by the Commission for such purpose.

(f) WITNESS ALLOWANCES AND FEES—

(1) IN GENERAL—The provisions of section 1821 of title 28, United States Code, shall apply to witnesses requested or subpoenaed to appear at any hearing of the Commission.

(2)   TRAVEL EXPENSES—The per diem and mileage allowances for witnesses shall be paid from funds available
to pay the expenses of the Commission.

Sec. 204. Commission Personnel Matters

(a)   COMPENSATION OF MEMBERS—Members of the
Commission shall serve without compensation for the
services of the member to the Commission.

(b)   TRAVEL EXPENSES—The members of the Commission
shall be allowed travel expenses, including per diem in
lieu of subsistence, at rates authorized for employees of
agencies under subchapter I of chapter 57 of title 5,
United States Code, while away from their homes or regular places of business in the performance of services for
the Commission.

(c)   STAFF—

(1)   IN GENERAL—The Chairperson of the Commission
may, without regard to the civil service laws and regula-
tions, appoint and terminate an executive director and
such other additional personnel as may be necessary to
enable the Commission to perform the duties of the
Commission.

(2)   EXECUTIVE DIRECTOR—The employment of an executive director shall be subject to confirmation by the
Commission.

(3)   COMPENSATION—The Chairperson of the Commission may fix the compensation of the executive director
and other personnel without regard to the provisions of
chapter 51 and subchapter III of chapter 53 of title 5,

United States Code, relating to classification of positions and General Schedule pay rates, except that the rate of pay for the executive director and other personnel may not exceed the rate payable for level V of the Executive Schedule under section 5316 of title 5.

(d)   DETAIL OF GOVERNMENT EMPLOYEES—Any Federal Government employee may be detailed to the Commission without reimbursement, and the detail shall be without interruption or loss of civil service status or privilege.

(e)   PROCUREMENT OF TEMPORARY AND INTERMITTENT SERVICES—The Chairperson of the Commission may procure temporary and intermittent services under section 3109(b) of title 5, United States Code, at rates for individuals which do not exceed the daily equivalent of the annual rate of basic pay prescribed for level V of the Executive Schedule under section 5316 of title 5.

Sec. 205. Termination of the Commission

The Commission shall terminate 90 days after the date on which the Commission submits its report under section 202.

Sec. 206. Funding

(a)   IN GENERAL—The Commission may expend an amount not to exceed $850,000, as provided by subsection (b), to carry out this title.

(b)   AVAILABILITY—Sums appropriated to the Department of Justice shall be made available to carry out this title.

FURTHER READING

Below is a selected—and by no means exhaustive—list of books and studies that illuminate key issues surrounding capital punishment in the United States.

History

Cesar Beccaria. *Of Crimes and Punishments.* Jane Grigson, translator; introduction by Mario Cuomo. Marsilio Publishers, 1996.

C. Brandon. *The Electric Chair: An Unnatural American History.* McFarland and Co., 1999.

Clarence Darrow. *Attorney for the Damned.* Arthur Weinberg, ed. Simon and Schuster, 1957.

Lawrence Friedman. *Crime and Punishment in American History.* Basic Books, 1993.

Peter Linebaugh. *The London Hanged: Crime and Civil Society in the Eighteenth Century.* Penguin, 1991.

Thomas Metzger. *Blood and Volts: Edison, Tesla and the Electric Chair.* Autonomedia, 1996.

The U.S. Supreme Court's historic opinions in *Furman* v. *Georgia*, *Gregg* v. *Georgia*, and other key capital-punishment cases are available online at supct.law.cornell.edu and other websites.

Deterrence

Hugo Adam Bedau, ed. *The Death Penalty in America: Current Controversies.* Oxford University Press, 1996.

James Gilligan, M.D. *Violence: Our Deadly Epidemic and Its Causes.* G.P. Putnam's Sons, 1996.

Victims, Vengeance, and Capital Punishment

Lt. Col. Dave Grossman. *On Killing.* Little Brown, 1995.

Judith Lois Herman. *Trauma and Recovery.* Basic Books, 1992.

Sister Helen Prejean. *Dead Man Walking: An Eyewitness Account of the Death Penalty in the United States.* Random House, 1993.

Capital Trials

Stephen Bright. "Counsel for the Poor: The Death Penalty not For the Worst Crime but the Worst Lawyer." *The Yale Law Journal,* May 1994. This and other reports by Bright, one of the nation's leading death-row appeals lawyers, are available online from the Southern Center for Human Rights at www.schr.org.

James Liebman. *A Broken System: Error Rates in Capital Cases, 1973–1995.* Columbia University School of Law, 2000. Available online from www.deathpenaltyinfo.org.

Michael Radalet, ed. *Facing the Death Penalty.* Temple University Press, 1989.

Austin Sarat. *When the State Kills.* Princeton University Press, 2001.

Innocence

Michael Mello. *The Wrong Man: A True Story of Innocence on Death Row.* University of Minnesota Press, 2001.

Gene Miller. *Invitation to a Lynching.* Random House, 1975.

Barry Scheck, Peter Neufeld, and Jim Dwyer. *Actual Innocence.* Doubleday, 2000.

Rob Warden and David Protess. *Gone in the Night.* Delacorte Press, 1993. Numerous reports and articles by the authors documenting death-row innocence cases are available online at www.centerforwrongfulconvictions.org.

C. Whitman et al. *Reasonable Doubts: Is the United States Executing Innocent People?* Quixote Center/Equal Justice USA, 2000. Available online at www.quixote.org.

Race and the Death Penalty

The most exhaustive information on this topic is available online from the Death Penalty Resource Center: www.deathpenalty info.org.

Religious Faith and Capital Punishment

James Megivern. *The Death Penalty: An Historical and Theolological Survey.* Paulist Press, 1997.

GETTING INVOLVED

Numerous national organizations provide information and resources to citizens seeking to get involved in ending the death penalty. Some of them are listed below. In addition, the Death Penalty Information Center (www.deathpenaltyinfo.org) and Equal Justice USA (www.quixote.org/ejusa), both provide information and links for numerous death-penalty moratorium groups at the state and local levels. If you are seeking to start a death-penalty moratorium campaign in your own community, all of these groups can provide crucial support material.

ACLU Capital Punishment Project
122 Maryland Ave., NE
Washington, DC 20002
www.aclu.org

Amnesty International—USA
Program to Abolish the Death Penalty
600 Pennsylvania Avenue, SE
Fifth Floor
Washington, DC 20003
202–544–0200
www.aiusa.org

Center on Wrongful Convictions

Northwestern University School of Law

357 East Chicago Avenue

Chicago, IL 60611

312–503–2391

www.centeronwrongfulconvictions.org

Citizens United for the Rehabilitation of Errants (CURE)

P.O. Box 2310

Washington, DC 20013

202–789–2126

Death Penalty Information Center

1320 Eighteenth Street, NW, 5th Floor

Washington, DC 20036

202–293–6970

www.deathpenaltyinfo.org

Equal Justice USA/Quixote Center

P.O. Box 5206

Hyattsville, MD 20782

301–699–0042

www.quixote.org/ejusa

Feminists for Life of America

733 15th St. NW , Suite 1100

Washington, DC 20005

202–737–3352

www.feministsforlife.org

Friends Committee on National Legislation

245 Second Street, NE

Washington, DC 20002

202–547–6000

www.fcnl.org

Human Rights Watch

1630 Connecticut Ave, NW

Suite 500

Washington, DC 20009

202–612–4321

www.hrw.org

Moratorium 2000

P.O. Box 13727

New Orleans, LA 70185

504–864–1071

www.Moratorium2000.org

Murder Victims Families for Reconciliation

2161 Mass. Ave

Cambridge, MA 02140

617–868–0007

www.mvfr.org

NAACP Legal Defense and Education Fund

99 Hudson St., 16th Floor

New York, NY 10013

800–221–7822

NAACP

4805 Mt. Hope Drive

Baltimore, MD 21215

410–521–4939

www.naacp.org

National Coalition to Abolish the Death Penalty

1436 U St., NW

Washington, DC 20009

202–387–3890

www.ncadp.org

Southern Center for Human Rights

83 Poplar St. NW

Atlanta, GA 30303

404–688–1202

www.schr.org

INDEX